GRASSROOTS ZEN

GRASSROOTS ZEN

MANFRED B. STEGER
AND PERLE BESSERMAN

TUTTLE PUBLISHING

BOSTON * RUTLAND, VERMONT * TOKYO

First published in 2001 by Tuttle Publishing, an imprint of Periplus Editions (HK) Ltd, with editorial offices at 153 Milk Street, Boston, Massachusetts 02109.

Library of Congress Cataloging-in-Publication Data
Besserman, Perle.
    Grassroots Zen / by Perle Besserman and Manfred B. Steger
        p. cm.
    ISBN 0-8048-3243-9
    1. Spiritual life — Zen Buddhism. 2. Zen Buddhism — Doctrines.
I. Steger, Manfred B., 1961 – II. Title.

Library of Congress Catalog Card Number:

  BQ9288 B48 2001
  294.3'444—dc21

Distributed by

USA
Tuttle Publishing
Distribution Center
Airport Industrial Park
364 Innovation Drive
North Clarendon, VT 05759-9436
Tel: (802) 773-8930
Tel: (800) 526-2778

Japan
Tuttle Shokai Ltd
1-21-13, Seki
Tama-ku, Kawasaki-shi
Kanagawa-ken 214-0022, Japan
Tel: (044) 833-0225
Fax: (044) 822-0413

Southeast Asia
Berkeley Books Pte Ltd
5 Little Road #08-01
Singapore 536983
Tel: (65) 280-1330
Fax: (65) 280-6290

First edition
06 05 04 03 02 01   10 9 8 7 6 5 4 3 2 1

Design by Gopa and the Bear ★ Printed in the United States of America

This book is dedicated to Uchiyama Gudo Roshi

and all the other victims

of fascism, militarism, and totalitarianism

in the twentieth century.

ACKNOWLEDGMENTS

We are grateful to the members of the Princeton Area Zen Group for making this book possible and particularly wish to thank those who generously permitted us to quote them.

For our lively Zen dialogues beyond Princeton, we'd like to thank Ursula Baatz, Wolfgang Waas, Jeff Shore, Michelle Mac-Donald, and Steve Smith.

CONTENTS

Suddenly I open up.
Everything settles down,
This blade of grass I call myself
Roots in the sounds
Honking geese, silence
Ticking clock
Incense smoke
Fading light
Wonderfully full.
I am a blade of grass,
Rooted here tonight
Grounded in these moments
Of wild bird flight.
It's here I claim my origin
And like a blade of grass
I bend and twist and live and die
In all that rushes past
Snow, ice, driving rain
Sun, stars
Pleasure, pain
Darkness, light
And on it goes with all of life.

Hetty Baiz

INTRODUCTION

TS'AO-PEN CH'AN

"Grassroots Zen" stems from the tenth- and eleventh-century Chinese Sung Dynasty's *ts'ao-pen ch'an* community meditation practice of householders, farmers, poets, artists, intellectuals, and business people. Without official sanction from Buddhist priests and beyond the monastery walls, such groups sprang up wherever committed, like-minded men and women gathered together to sit in meditation. Ts'ao-pen ch'an is the original stock, the form of Zen transplanted from the East, that successfully took root in twentieth-century Western soil. This lay Zen tradition parallels the development of Zen outside the monastery in Sung China. Because there is no formal lineage, no hierarchy, and no listing of names of masters, it isn't as easily documented as monastic Zen but falls into the realm of social history. It's Zen without the religious trappings. It's proof that Zen meditation can be practiced no matter where, when, or with whom it finds itself.

The self-reliant approach of Grassroots Zen appeals no less to Westerners at the threshold of the twenty-first century than it did to the ancient Chinese. Although we aren't monks or nuns, or even Buddhists, we share the hunger for answers to the same lifelong questions: "Who am I?" "Why do I have to die?" "Why do I suffer?" Like our Chinese "grassroots" forebears, we don't need official religious sanction to look for answers to these questions. We only need to sit down together and meditate with people like ourselves—practical-minded, no-frills people who share the experience of juggling career, family life, and social responsibility along with their deep commitment to Zen.

GRASSROOTS ZEN TODAY

Rooted in a spiritual partnership model based on "power sharing," today's Grassroots Zen practice emphasizes gender equality and family practice, and is oriented toward children, work, and social engagement. It can be practiced by any person — religious or not—who is committed to self-realization and who is willing to make meditation a serious concern rather than a fleeting hobby. It encourages the sharing of responsibility and democratic decision making. Hence, community policy is democratically discussed and implemented rather than handed down from above.

Grassroots Zen is not an isolated, metaphysical practice cut off from the world; it integrates meditation and daily life in the busy marketplace beyond the monastery. Here its real challenge is to make us ever more aware of the interdependence of all beings and to help us put this insight into practice by connecting the political, social, and spiritual dimensions of our existence. The unity of being experienced in Zen meditation must be expressed in the world as openness, nonviolence, compassion, friendship, and democracy.

For the layperson in particular, spiritual insight means integrating the realization of the interdependence of all things with the way we live and act in the world. When meditation reveals to us that we are ourselves no different from the noisy neighbor next door, the homeless woman in the park, or the spotted owl, social and ethical engagement become second nature. This is the kind of Zen practice that is synonymous with "life Zen practice" in the world we occupy right here and now. Following the compassionate way of the *bodhisattva*—one who gives up personal liberation to attend to this world and the suffering of its many beings—Grassroots Zen practitioners must likewise reject the empty perfection of *nirvana* (Sanskrit term for the "extinguishing" of all desire) for our tumultuous arena of time, space, and motion. Unlike other spiritual or religious disciplines that depend on outside intervention from a god or transmission from a master, Grassroots Zen places responsibility squarely on the shoulders of the individual practitioner. It is we who decide to sit in daily meditation and attend meditation retreats while simultaneously holding down a job, caring for children and aging parents, voting, volunteering, saving the planet. Like the Buddha—who is said to be practicing still—we too are invited each moment of our lives to embark upon the path. Fortunately, we no longer have to travel far from home to find it.

OUR STORY

Since everything in this book is based on our own experience as Zen practitioners and teachers, we'd like to tell you how we came to Grassroots Zen. Before becoming co-teachers at the Princeton Area Zen Group in Princeton, New Jersey, in 1991, we each spent ten years practicing Zen. Half those years were dedicated to hard traditional training with Japanese monks and the remainder in Hawai'i with lay teacher Robert Aitken Roshi, the "Dean of American Zen Masters." Inspired to take lay Zen practice a step further away from its Japanese roots, we started—on moving from Hawai'i to Princeton—a little Zen group and began experimenting with a more American "grassroots" version of the practice. Our experience in Hawai'i made it clear that it was religious escapism that led us to dress up in black robes and pretend we were Japanese monks. After trying for so long to fit this image of "tradition," we could no longer avoid the fact that we were Westerners living in the late twentieth century. As humanists and "progressives," we were concerned with civil rights, racial equality, economic justice, nonviolence, ecology, and feminism. We were bothered by the patriarchal and hierarchical nature of traditional Japanese Zen, its militarism, and its distance from social action and "real world" concerns. As witnesses to our genocidal century, we could no longer close our eyes and ears to the violent racism of some of our most revered Japanese Zen masters. Our "samurai Zen" karma had clearly come to an end.

It was particularly disturbing to see women and men once deeply committed to Zen practice giving it up because they found it increasingly "irrelevant" to their lives. We saw our task as twofold: make Zen more palatable to Western lay practitioners and do this while remaining true to the "heart" of the practice. Dispensing with the feudal cultural style of Japanese Zen in our Princeton community, we retained what we felt were its essential elements: *zazen*, formal sitting meditation; *sesshin*, silent meditation retreats; *dharma* talks, practice-related lectures given by Zen teachers; *koans*, verbal exchanges between teacher and student that are designed to facilitate spiritual insight; and *dokusan*, private, practice-related teacher-student interviews.

We eliminated monastic robes and tonsure, as well as every vestige of militarism and male dominance inherent in Japanese Zen training. This is especially important, given the centuries-old subordination of women in most world religions, including traditional Zen Buddhism. Imported from Japan in the 1950s, Zen was perfectly compatible with the traditional patterns of male domination it found in its new home in the West. Combining principles and training rooted in images of male transcendence and female materiality, it glorified celibacy and demonized the body. Thus, even those women who sought to escape their lower status by becoming nuns remained excluded from the hierarchy. Many women silently endured sexual and psychological humiliation and abuse in order to be accepted into the sangha (Buddhist community).

Gradually, as the abuses came to light, greater numbers of women were sufficiently emboldened to question not only the relationship between Zen teachers and their disciples, but also the patriarchal structures that shaped the practice itself. By the 1980s, spreading from the West even to the farthest, most entrenched misogynistic strongholds of Asian monasticism, the women's movement had spawned a new stage in the post-war spiritual revolution. In the new era, emphasis was placed less on looking to a Zen master or lineage for legitimacy than on taking responsibility for one's own practice and trusting one's own experience. Feminist challenges to male Zen teachers were extended to questioning status, androcentric images and symbols, and teaching styles. Inspired by this feminist paradigm, we shaped a more holistic, inclusive form of Zen practice in our Princeton sangha.

The Princeton Area Zen Group (PAZG)

Within three years, the little Grassroots Zen group in Princeton had grown large enough to rent a permanent space and start collecting membership dues instead of relying on contributions. In flyers, the Princeton Area Zen Group advertised itself as "a community of like-minded people who practice Zen meditation together every Sunday evening and are equally responsible for maintaining and supporting the *zendo*—the 'place of practice.'" Longer meditation retreats were held, beginners' nights were set aside for introducing Zen to newcomers, and, as the group's co-teachers, we went out into the

Princeton community giving Zen talks, workshops, and semi-
nars, as well as making connections with local Jewish and
Christian clergy interested in acquainting themselves and their
congregations with the practice of meditation.

We based our Grassroots Zen community on a shared commitment to meditation practice and friendship. The Greek phi-
losopher Socrates once called such feelings of respect and bonds
of friendship *philia*—an idea that has been losing its appeal in
our alienated mass society. Because the practice of *philia* is possible only in a small, decentralized setting, we decided jointly to
keep our group limited in size and outreach.

PAZG Members

Inspired by the secular atmosphere and pragmatic language of
Grassroots Zen, members of PAZG—whether calling themselves Unitarians, devout Catholics, ethnic Jews, or religious
unaffiliateds—gradually created a comfortable blend of Eastern
and Western Zen practice. No one objected to having an altar
and putting a picture of the Buddha on it, or using incense, bells,
and traditional Japanese floor cushions. At the same time, the
relaxed, nonhierarchical relationship between teachers and students, the personal friendships developing among members, and
the intimacy shared by everyone involved in the group's growing pains made for a spiritual sense of purpose and a communal
loyalty that precluded any sectarian squabbling. Regardless of
occupation, gender, nationality, age, or social status, none of the
members saw Zen as an exotic Asian import that might alienate
them from their "real life" situations or surroundings. Including
nonpracticing spouses, inviting children and other family members and friends to dinners and potluck parties after weekend
retreats, and extending social contact beyond the Zen group into
the community even served to attract local townspeople who
initially feared that a cult might be sprouting up in their midst.

The fact that neither teachers nor group members wore black robes or shaved their heads (a monastic tradition still practiced in many American lay Zen centers) also helped in connecting PAZG to the social and intellectual life beyond the zendo.

As Grassroots Zen teachers, we welcomed a membership consisting largely of beginners with no previous Zen experience and no prejudices about Zen practice. No one asked whether the kind of sitting meditation being taught was Japanese or American, old or new. The physicists, environmentalists, artists, students, homemakers, accountants, poets, government workers, retirees, and therapists who joined the group were less interested in questions of hierarchy, "lineage," and other "Cathedral Zen" issues than they were in actually sitting down on their meditation cushions and experiencing the "Buddha Way" for themselves. And because the ancient Chinese practice of meditating on koans was continuously related to their own daily life experience, members took to it easily.

The fact that we were a husband-and-wife team who carried no symbols of religious authority—and were not supported by the group but earned our living like everyone else—also helped to relax the clerical, and overridingly masculine, atmosphere long associated with Zen. Student-teacher interviews (minus the elaborate prostrations and monastic formalities of traditional Asian Zen) opened new lines of communication that otherwise might have been obscured by time and cultural differences, and meditation retreats in which all members were equally responsible for organizing, financing, and carrying out practical tasks served to create a more democratic form of Zen practice. Discipline—a Zen bugaboo in our increasingly egalitarian age—did not have to be symbolized by the long wooden stick used in monasteries. Most PAZG members were responsible adult professionals with children of their own to discipline; some were white-haired seniors, and it seemed inappropriate to walk around the zendo hitting them on the back with a stick to keep them awake. The product of the group's increasing inclination to "feminize" Zen, a posture check was implemented instead, and those who could not sit cross-legged on floor cushions were taught how to sit zazen in a chair.

After five years, we left the Princeton area for academic jobs in Illinois. Meeting several times throughout the year for meditation retreats; communicating via monthly taped dharma talks and group discussions, telephone, mail, and e-mail; and designating teachers' assistants from among the membership, both we and our students now embarked on a new phase in our ongoing "grassroots" experiment. To everyone's surprise, instead of signaling the group's demise, the absence of resident teachers brought the members even closer. By undertaking responsibility for weekly sittings and maintaining the zendo entirely on their own, in addition to financing and arranging retreats, creating a Web site, and publishing an occasional *Crazy Cloud Sangha Newsletter*, which publicized the group and introduced new members to the rudiments of meditation, the Princeton Area Zen Group proved that an independent, egalitarian, and socially engaged form of American Grassroots Zen was indeed possible.

Role Plurality

To be a Western lay Zen teacher at the beginning of the twenty-first century means to accept what we call "role plurality." As the infamous Zen scandals of the 1980s in the United States have shown, the traditional role of the roshi (Zen master) as the living manifestation of enlightenment tended to encourage students to extend the role of the "master" to all other aspects of human existence. They assumed that their teachers could do no wrong. Even clearly immoral actions such as heavy drinking or sexual abuse on the part of the *roshi* were seen as "mysterious teachings" too advanced for "ordinary" practitioners to understand. Such an automatic translation of the special role of the "master" to all areas of life kept students from realizing that their teachers weren't perfect. As human beings, we all have many different roles as well as individual strengths and weaknesses. In some roles, we are called upon to lead; in others, we must follow more experienced people. An acceptance of the plurality of our roles means that qualified Zen teachers ought to be able to lead their students in meditation, but that they, in turn, must also be willing to learn from their students in other areas. In other words, both students and teachers must allow themselves to assume different roles in shifting situations, and let go of preconceived, petrified hierarchies that threaten to undermine the fluidity of human interaction.

As Grassroots Zen teachers, we always felt the need to develop close friendships with our students. We didn't want to be confined to the role of the infallible roshi, and we refused to receive payment for our services. We wanted to be able to go for a cup of coffee with our students and be seen as equal conversation partners. We wanted to be able to invite students to dinner and have open discussions about politics, careers, and cultural issues in an atmosphere of equality conducive to a free exchange of ideas. In this spirit, we're practicing not only as Zen teachers but also as householders, wage earners, family members, friends, and citizens, equally engaged in protesting the construction of another polluting mega-hog farm in our Central Illinois town as in guiding our Princeton students in meditation. In offering this kind of Zen teaching to a small group of people who, like ourselves, were searching for peace of mind in the midst of hectic activity, we found our home in Zen's *ts'ao-pen ch'an* heritage.

THE ROOT OF IT ALL

In this book, we'll be exploring the issues confronting today's Grassroots Zen practitioners. Taking a "hands-on" approach, we'll show how the social, professional, and psychological concerns of ordinary people can provide opportunities for spiritual awakening. Using the metaphor of a "grassy field" for today's Western ts'ao-pen ch'an *sangha* (an egalitarian community of socially mobile members who place less emphasis on transmission and hierarchy than on individual responsibility), we will focus on the interplay between the "field" (the Zen community), the single "grass root" (the individual practitioner), and the dimensions of "time, space, and motion" (the world). At the surface level, each community member appears in the world of time, space, and motion as a separate self with a unique role, a single blade of grass emerging from a single root. The individual grass root and blade are one, each dependent on the other. The root is implicit in the blade; the blade is potential in the root. But when we dig deeper into the soil, we find that the individual grass root is actually being sustained, sheltered, and nurtured by all the other grass roots in the field. *Grassroots Zen* can be seen as a "gardener's guide" for discovering the true nature of the self in that connection.

Like the single blade of grass in the field, the self is part of a great seamless web of life. Its duration in time is seasonal, subject to changing conditions. It is rooted in the earth, but not permanently. Meditation reveals that the true nature of the interdependent self is compassion. It dwells without clinging; when rain comes, it is fully one with rain; when the sun appears, it is fully one with the sun.

The present moment is the root of it all. Sad or happy, moving or at rest, the moment provides endless opportunities for cultivating awareness. Each root in our grassy field, each moment is filled with all the nutrients we need. Going to the root, becoming one with the moment, we discover that life is perfect as it is. We are, at last, at home in the world.

Zazen (meditation) is the way to realizing the true nature of the self. Seeing beyond the tip of the single blade of grass and its root family, we realize that there is only change. What we imagine as a solid block of experience called "time" is actually the self in continuous motion. In whatever form it appears, the self is at one with change. We ourselves are transforming with the moment, manifesting now as grass root, now as sun, now as sky. We are simultaneously unique and indistinguishable from what our ancient Chinese forebears called "the world of the ten thousand things."

In its deepest sense, Grassroots Zen is about going to the root, discovering that everything just is. Standing confidently on our own ground, we are at home with this realization. Everything *is*; whatever happens, *is*—including all the terrible things and all the wonderful things. Centered in this root wisdom, we are free to move through our lives. Without this root wisdom, however, there is only suffering. We suffer because we don't accept the moment that is here, right now, exactly as it presents itself. We want to avoid it. We reject it, we try to escape it, but how can we, when we ourselves *are*, at this very moment, one with the root itself? When we're one with it, we know what to do. The ego disappears and the choices open up: we find ourselves walking a straight path on which we confidently take the next step.

TIME, SPACE, AND MOTION

Like the self, the grass root is temporary, subject to seasonal changes. It interacts with wind, rain, sun, and snow, and changes from moment to moment. Its brief duration in time makes these interactions all the more precious. Whether coming as drought, hail, and killing frost or as sunny warmth and refreshing rain, time is a vital element in our grassroots field of practice. Meditation is synonymous with cultivating the field. It reveals that the only way for the self to thrive is by disappearing into the changing conditions thrust up by time.

Given our fiercely individualistic sense of self and the frantic pace of our times, how does the grassroots practitioner integrate the timeless world of zazen with the timebound activities of daily life? The first section of the book, "Time," addresses this question by exploring what it means to "become one with the moment."

The second section, "Space," explores how we can stake out a place for the self in the world. In addition to examining what we commonly call "good" and "bad" spaces, it shows how zazen balances the needs of the self within its spatial limitations. Like time, space, too, is temporary, and our little patch of ground is always changing, so finding the Middle Way is essential. This section of the book will show how to manage the self without choking it or letting it run wild.

"Motion," the third section of the book, is about what it takes to achieve the balance between practice and daily life. Focusing on the individual and communal rhythms of the self, we'll describe a variety of situations that call for yielding or persisting, connecting or letting go, speeding up or slowing down.

We would like to close this introduction with a word of advice: Grassroots Zen cannot be practiced without daily sitting meditation. Twenty-five minutes of focusing on the breath is indispensable for establishing a meaningful spiritual practice. For those readers who have not yet begun to sit, we offer this book as a pointer toward the path. We hope that those who already meditate will be inspired by our words to deepen their practice.

time

SO COME, SO GONE

COMING TO TERMS WITH CHANGE

In its scant, poignant depictions of the changing seasons, Japanese haiku perfectly captures the nature of our "hollyhock journey" along the "invisible road." Whether appearing as golden sun or as grey rain, the change inherent in passing time is a relentless reminder of our fleeting "grassroots" existence. We don't know where we came from or where we're going, but we never want to stop. We cling for dear life to our little patch of ground, yet the more we cling, the more we suffer. We just can't seem to make peace with changing conditions. Only when we find ourselves out of breath and unable to go on, do we come to a stop. One day it hits us that change is inescapable. Change means there's nothing to hold onto. Change is what brings us to Zen practice.

EVERY BREATH IS DIFFERENT

Nowhere does change become more evident than when we sit on our cushions following the breath. Because we don't usually pay attention to what feels like an automatic process, we fall into the illusion that our breaths are all the same. We think only opera singers and asthmatics have to be aware of breathing. Suddenly we notice that every breath is different, that each inhalation and exhalation is unique and unrepeatable. Broadening our attention, we look at our hearing, touching, seeing, tasting, and smelling and notice that they too are unreplicable. Each step we take, each morsel we taste, each sound we hear is unlike any other. Jolted out of our stupor, we find everything is changing, unfolding from moment to moment. Over and over again, yet always fresh and new, never stale, never routine, we ourselves are coming and going as change.

This isn't a one-time realization. It must be experienced anew every time we sit down on our cushions. We tend to sink back into our old mental habits, so we keep returning to the breath, to this changing moment. We need to allow ourselves to let change happen. Only when we realize that the universe is itself nothing but change, and that it's going on all the time, can we begin to experience ourselves as change.

CLOSING THE GAP

Meditation abates the fear of change. It loosens our clutch on the wish for permanence. We no longer take refuge in the idea of an essential soul, an everlasting identity tag that's perfect, unmoving, unchangeable, and therefore "real." The self at one with change is more like a drop of water flowing over a rock, changing shape and form as it assumes the face of the rock, perhaps stopping from time to time, until it grows dense and is once again pulled down by gravity into the stream from which it came.

Really allowing yourself to become one with change means you no longer think about change. Instead of separating yourself from changing conditions, emotions, expectations, and goals, you simply disappear into them. They're always new. Life is never boring. Having closed the gap between the changing universe, the moment, and the separate entity you think of as your "self," you can at last come and go in peace.

PRACTICING THE ART OF CHANGE

There's a wonderful Pali term for the Buddha, *Tathagata*. Literally translated, it means "so come, so gone." In other words, Buddha is nothing but change. Always present, the *Tathagata* is continuously manifesting the many things of this world. Nothing is excluded, nothing is separate from this bountiful harvest. Everything is change. When we sit zazen, we practice the art of change, getting a whole new perspective on the passing of time. Instead of fearing change, we can even begin to enjoy our changing conditions. Growing older, letting go of children, reuniting with friends from far away—all these are part of our practice, part of us. We are continuously changing and being changed, living as change. Any condition, no matter how painful or joyful, inevitably gives way to another. But it's only by immersing ourselves in the moment that we fully realize this, experiencing over and over again what it is to grow and unfold.

It all begins with the breath. Inhaling this moment, exhaling the next. When you drift away, just bring yourself back. This is what's happening right here. Now. The last breath is gone; here's a new one. A thought comes, fine. Let it pass through. Gone. Back to the breath. Inhale. Exhale. Another thought comes. Okay, too. Let it pass through. The brain generates thoughts in the same way that the liver generates bile. That's the way the brain works. That's the brain's job. You don't sit and worry about your liver doing what it's supposed to do.

You don't get angry with it. Apply the same easy acceptance to the function of your brain. Let it send up thoughts. Just don't get carried away by them. Don't get too interested in them. At the same time, allow them to come and go, without monitoring yourself. Eventually, mind and breath become one. This is the quickest entry into discovering yourself as change.

Chinese traditional doctors believe that breath and mind are connected. Those of us who've had acupuncture treatments have experienced this firsthand. As soon as the needles are placed at the meridian points, you simultaneously feel your breath and your thoughts slowing down. The mind actually starts to relax. That's why so many patients fall asleep. It's even better for patients who meditate; instead of falling asleep, they go into a relaxed but alert state that helps the body attend to healing.

Just breathing. Nothing more. Yet the experience of just sitting and attending to the breath brings us back to the basic fact of our existence. It's not that we're illusory. That's a mistaken idea some people have about Zen practice—that there isn't anyone there at all. You only have to slam your finger in a door to know that's not true. There's a difference between illusoriness and transience, though. The self, like everything else in the universe, comes and goes, isn't fixed, isn't ever the same from moment to moment. When we're hurt, we bleed real blood and cry real tears. But only momentarily. That's the self being hurt now. In the space of a moment, it will be transformed, become totally new. The self is real, manifesting as the changing moment. The only illusion is that the self is solid, fixed, and that change is somehow assaulting it from the outside.

Real intimacy with change means we don't automatically cling to the "lovely" moments and reject the "ugly" ones. Rain comes, we're soaked with rain; sun comes, we're soaked with sun. That's all.

Zen people often talk about "accepting the moment as it is." That's okay, but what we like even better is "caring for the moment" with the same lavish tenderness you'd bestow on a newborn. Cici, a nurse-midwife acquaintance of ours, is a perfect example of what we mean. On call at all hours of the day and night, she may get tired, but she's never bored by her practice. Privileged to be bringing newborn life into the world, Cici devotes equal attention and care to every baby she delivers. It's the same with Zen practice. Once you've experienced each moment on your cushions as "newborn," how can you not treat it with care?

DON'T BE USED BY THE TWENTY-FOUR HOURS

SPECIAL MOMENTS

Time is the grid human beings impose on change. It's the way we Westerners in particular measure "progress." Even though Einstein has told us otherwise, we still picture time "marching on" in a straight line toward some destined goal. We see it as a friend when it's "on our side" or when we can "buy ourselves" some, or as an enemy when it's "against us" or when we "run out of it." Knowing that death will inevitably cut our "time line," we spend most of our lives denying it, pretending we'll go on "forever." In other words, we are captive to our own self-created illusion of permanence.

We go through our daily routines creating special moments and discarding the time in between. When we're not enjoying those special moments, we want to move on quickly—but we can't, because we're carrying time like a dead weight. We want to be done with that annoying chore and hurry on to our lunch break or our favorite television show. We want the drudgery of the week to end so that the weekend will come.

Then we can lock ourselves away in the workshop and putter all day long, or maybe relax in the recliner with a beer and do nothing. But when the weekend comes, we want it to be Thursday, because we go bowling Thursday nights, and so it goes. Setting up these special moments, time's little stolen pleasures, makes life bearable. Looking forward to the time that isn't here yet becomes the "natural" thing to do.

The problem is that the special moments don't seem to be in as abundant supply as the not-so-special ones. As soon as our special moment is over, we must create another one, and another, and another. Always chasing after these moments, consuming them, greedily taking them in without even chewing or digesting them, we're like the legendary Chinese hungry ghosts, devouring imaginary food and never feeling full. There's no rest. Pushing ourselves like this makes us edgy. We get angry with people for getting in the way of those special moments. We get angry at ourselves and push even harder. Soon we start to hate the hours that somehow have to be filled, the ones that aren't special. We develop little tricks to avoid them; we live in dreams, projections, memories. We don't want to deal with what's going on now, because it's not exciting. It doesn't feel good. Living like this, we never really find fulfillment, because there's no stopping to ease the mind of its burdensome task.

STANDING TIME ON ITS HEAD

In one of his famous talks, the great Chinese Zen master Chao-Chou admonished his monks, saying, "Don't be used by the twenty-four hours." If Chao-Chou's monks needed a reminder not to be used by time, imagine how much more difficult it is for today's Grassroots Zen practitioner. Chao-Chou's words may inspire us, but we must put them into practice if we really want to experience the true nature of time for ourselves.

The way we see it, Chao-Chou is saying that we've got to turn time upside down if we want to stop being used by the twenty-four hours. We have to make a radical change in perspective and start looking at life in a whole new way. Only when we stand time on its head will we be able to see that *every single moment is special*!

Anyone doing a headstand knows how different time feels in that upside-down position. You can't go anywhere and you've got to steady yourself to keep from falling over. You literally have to come to a full stop. In this unaccustomed position, you have no choice but to pay attention to what's going on, otherwise you might topple over. Gradually, everything in the room, including your body, becomes one with the living moment. The clock on the wall reads three, but on the other hand, it could also be a quarter past twelve. Is that twelve noon or twelve midnight? Standing on your head, it's impossible to tell. What's more, it doesn't really matter. You are too absorbed in every little vein on the leaf of that rose in the upside-down vase on the upside-down coffee table to care what time it is. Or maybe going eye to eye with that little red spider on the floor in front of you is the most important thing you could be doing with your time.

It's the same with sitting zazen on your cushion. Only instead of standing on your head, meditating reverses your relationship to time by shutting down your "special moments" machine and bringing you to a full stop. Once you've stopped, every single moment, whatever it's made of, becomes an adventure. Life is suddenly interesting because each moment invites you to participate in what's going on right now. You become totally absorbed in the moment, submerged in its radiant "suchness." Bathed in the powerful glow of your attention, every mundane activity becomes special; picking up a pen and filling out a form become "enlightened" acts. Instead of carrying time around like a dead weight or dreading it as something to be gotten over with, you actually start enjoying yourself as you disappear into your chores. What used to be boring becomes light, shiny, brand new. Your mood becomes light and shiny too. There's a new respect for the "little things" you tended to overlook before. As you let more of the world in, you begin to interact more generously with other people. No longer obsessed with your own special moments, you find yourself actually listening to that colleague at the coffee machine as she describes her trip to Tuscany.

MICRO-ZEN MOMENTS

We feel more poised and confident as the old adversarial relationship with time disappears and we enter the "timeless" realm of the moment. We go about our daily routines with a peaceful mind. There are no extraneous activities, no additional duties to fulfill in order to get somewhere else. Even obstacles become opportunities for realizing ourselves in the moment. The deeper our attention, the more vivid the moment. Relieved of its grid, time melts into change.

Becoming one with the changing conditions of the moment is like becoming one with our breath when we sit. The only difference is that we're focusing on daily activity as our practice, eliminating the artificial barrier between the zendo and the marketplace. Practice isn't just what we do on the cushions; it's what we do on the cushions *and* everywhere else in the course of the twenty-four hours—but not as a duty or a chore, something extra that we must fit into our lives. Of course nobody succeeds in being attentive one hundred percent of the time, but, as one of our Japanese Zen teachers used to say, "Five percent very good!" You just keep trying, and when you fail, there's no need to blame yourself. There's always the next moment.

Sitting regularly reminds us to return to right now when we start straying in pursuit of that special moment. And even when we're not sitting formally, it's possible to bring that "re-minding" into our busy lives by practicing what we call "micro-Zen moments." Here's how to do it.

When you feel you're pushing yourself, chasing after an imaginary goal or a special moment, just sit back and take a breath. Let everything go. After a few breaths, you'll notice that you're already right in the middle of your special moment. Sit back, gaze out the window, and let the light bathe you. Let the sounds become one with your breath. Relax completely into your surroundings, and it's a sure bet you'll experience that special moment. There's no need to chase after it, only to open up to it at any time, *because it's always here!* Practice often enough and these micro-Zen moments will become as natural as brushing your teeth or having your cup of morning tea.

AN END TO SUFFERING

Being present to the moment allows us to rest in the dynamic unfolding of being—not as separate, isolated individuals, but as the universe itself. It's what the Buddha meant when he said, "Below the heavens, above the earth—only I, alone in the universe." This may sound philosophical, but the way the Buddha got to that understanding was very pragmatic. He simply sat down under a tree and meditated. Driven to search for an answer to suffering, he discovered neither the end of pain nor a void that too often passes for "enlightenment" but the end of suffering. He no longer experienced himself as an atomistic, isolated self that's battered around by time. Suffering dissipates when we no longer make meditation another "special moment" on the cushion, but live it twenty-four hours a day.

Seeing that everything we could ever want is already here transforms the world into our grassy field of practice. Living consciously as we come and go immediately translates into peace of mind. Everything else grows from there: Confidence. Poise. Joy. Understanding. Tolerance. Openness. Interdependence. Compassion. Sympathy. That's the Zen ethic: not a set of commandments etched in stone, but a mind freer than air and more fluid than water. Just the myriad blades of grass, bending in the wind. Can you feel it?

DWELLING IN TIME

A VIRTUAL WORLD

We were recently sitting in a café in the lobby of a newly-opened cineplex, having a cup of coffee. While waiting for our film to begin, we watched a couple pass our table. They had just come out of one of the theaters together and were holding hands, but the woman was talking to someone else on a cell phone. It was a weird sight. Here was a woman engaging in conversation with someone who wasn't there while holding hands with a man she was ignoring. It set us to thinking about how people spend their time in an increasingly "virtual" world, one in which our immediate experience of the moment is being overtaken by gadgets. In the twenty-first century, dwelling in that timeless "garden where the camellia-tree opens its whiteness" will take a lot more effort. In order to clear our way through the weeds, we'll have to make more time for meditation retreats.

Sesshin

Zen retreats, or *sesshin*, are orchestrated to help us concentrate on the experience of the moment, on what it is to be alive in this world, right now. By living for three, four, or five days together in silence—away from the telephone, our jobs, our families, newspapers, books, television, radio, and car—we truly come to know the unencumbered joy of seeing, smelling, tasting, touching, hearing, and thinking. Meditating, eating, sleeping, and walking in silence teach us the wonder of dwelling lightly in time. It's similar to that good feeling we get when we clean out a closet: we get rid of all the junk we don't need or use and that serves no purpose but to collect dust and attract moths. It's the opposite of the letdown you get when you buy something. Maybe you're excited about what you bought for a day or two, but usually after a week, it doesn't excite you anymore. That's because shopping is often used to fill an emptiness inside. People shop to ease their loneliness and to find "community." They shop to escape the buzzing chatter in their minds, which is also the reason people glue themselves to their cell phones or keep their television sets on all day. They're afraid of the silence and afraid of the void in their hearts.

In sesshin, the more you let go, the better you feel. It's common, in fact, for people not to want sesshin to end. The first day is usually hard; you're still shaking off the dust of the world, still have one foot in the zendo and the other outside in the busy life you've left behind. But soon enough, you are immersed in the silent delights of the "garden where the camellia-tree opens its whiteness." Time flies by. Each period of zazen leaves you feeling lighter. There's a sense of completion in that feeling, of everything being perfect as it is without any need for ornamentation or embellishment. If it's autumn and the "camellia-tree" is shedding its leaves, you don't feel sad that it isn't spring. So it is with the mind. There's no need to sweep away thoughts, merely to unburden yourself of the baggage they carry with them. There's no need to pile them up or to collect them, either. If they're autumn thoughts, let them be autumn thoughts. Let them fall. Meet everything that comes into your path with an uncluttered mind.

LIKE A CLOUD OVER WATER

In Japanese, the word for Zen monk is *unsui*, or "cloud-water." It means living like a cloud over water, traveling with no worldly possessions and leaving no traces. For the Grassroots Zen practitioner, it means living very lightly on the earth, unburdened by extraneous possessions, concepts, habits, and fears. Traditionally, becoming a monk meant leaving home and joining a monastic community. But how do we householders practice "home leaving?" What does it mean to live like a cloud over water in the midst of our grassy field of family, work, school, freeways, taxes?

To begin with, we can "leave home" every morning or evening when we sit zazen. By taking leave of our cluttered lives and entering the path to our "true home" in every breath, our true home is always with us. We can't buy this home from a realtor; we don't need to shop for it. It only appears to be beyond our reach when we bury it under a mountain of stale notions. We've got to cut through this mountain in order for our true home to reveal itself.

Frequently depicted in Buddhist art as idealized figures, archetypal bodhisattvas represent women and men who have postponed their own liberation from suffering for the sake of helping others. On every traditional Zen altar, there are two bodhisattva statues. On one side, there's Kannon, the bod-hisattva of compassion. On the other, there's Manjusri, the sword-wielding slayer of delusions. With one swift blow, his sword cuts through the mountain of mental clutter that keeps us from our true home. Kannon and Manjusri are really one and the same; they manifest the two faces of compassionate wisdom wielded by the bodhisattva—that is, by us, when we sit down and meditate. There is no compassion distinct from cutting through; there is no cutting through without compassion.

When we clutter our minds and our lives, we are not dwelling compassionately in time. We learned this firsthand when we joined an organic food cooperative run by local farmers in Central Illinois. As city people accustomed to shopping in supermarkets for produce, we were disappointed when we got tomatoes only three or four months in spring and summer and when we couldn't get imported cherries or strawberries in winter. A visit to the farm and a little education from the organic farmers taught us about the "unnaturalness" of growing things out of season, of how much the soil suffered from the planting of fruits and vegetables that weren't compatible with the time and region. Suddenly, the fact that the soil was a living thing became real, and compassion for the earth more than just a metaphor. The proof of the pudding was in the eating. We began to notice that when we craved fruits and vegetables out of season and, bypassing the co-op, bought them elsewhere, they tasted strange. Tomatoes tasted like potatoes; peaches tasted more like apples—especially now that the genetic engineers have gotten into the act. What a pleasure it was to bite into a piece of organic melon straight from the farm—in season! What a difference in taste! It was an excellent lesson in living lightly, like a cloud over water, right here in our grassroots world.

INSIDE AND OUTSIDE ARE ONE

When we clutter our minds, we are not being compassionate toward ourselves. When we clutter the earth with products borne of our desires regardless of the season, we are not being compassionate toward the universe. "Inside and outside are one," goes the Zen saying. What we do and think and buy and eat aren't done in a vacuum. When we sit on our cushions and clutter our minds with the poisons of greed, hatred, and ignorance, when we don't meet and honor the moment, we cheat ourselves of truly living—not just lightly in the economic sense, but also in the sense of being truly alive. We are wracked by our heavy burden of acquisitiveness. Worry, too, is a form of acquisitiveness that reveals itself when we collect grievances, harbor envy, and fixate on venomous feelings toward those we feel have injured us. We unnecessarily add to our suffering when we ruminate about the past and fantasize about the future. All this stuff in the closet of the mind keeps us from treading the earth lightly; we have to pick our way through a mountain of junk—both inside and outside. Life itself becomes an obstacle. When the mind is filled with accumulated thoughts and worn-out desires or fantasies, we can't confront situations and people clearly, whether at home or at the office.

Zazen is the activity of continuously clearing out the mind. It leaves us free to go into the world unburdened, clear-eyed, and light. Meeting the moment, we carry nothing extraneous. Like the cloud over water, we leave no tracks. Freed of those possessions by which we are ourselves "possessed," we can truly taste the delicious fruits of the season. Just twenty-five minutes of zazen a day is enough.

THE OAK TREE STANDS

NOBLE ON THE HILL

EVEN IN

CHERRY BLOSSOM TIME

BASHŌ

RIGHT TIMING

DHARMA DANCING

Most of us associate Buddhist equanimity with the serenely smiling statues of Buddha seen in museums, so we think enlightened people must always be perfectly tranquil. But every now and then, in those same museums, we encounter a totally different version of Buddhist equanimity; it might be a scroll featuring a buck-toothed fellow in a shabby robe wielding a broom or a statue of a thick-necked, fierce-eyed monk leaping with joy at the moment of spiritual awakening. Unlike the ethereal, transcendent Buddhas, these fellows are rooted in the earth, alive. Their eyes are open; their bodies appear to be moving. You'd swear they were breathing. Here is Zen equanimity at work in this grassroots world, "even in cherry blossom time."

It's unlikely that we'll ever attain the serenity of the ancient Buddhas. But it's said that the Buddha himself is still practicing, so we can take heart. And like the Buddha, we have to work with what we've got. No matter where in life we find ourselves situated, the practice is endless. It's not just a question of one blissful burst of enlightenment—no matter how great or small. It's a question of continued practice, of applying what we do on our cushions in every area of life—experienced sometimes as joy, sometimes as failure; sometimes as gain and sometimes as loss. Practice consists of becoming one with this ceaselessly changing life-flow. It's interacting with the cashier at the supermarket checkout counter, the mail carrier, the bus driver, the guy at the newspaper kiosk, the woman who fixes our latte-to-go in the morning as we head to work. This is our own particular Grassroots Zen rhythm.

It's hard to find equanimity in this swiftly flowing current of contemporary life. We don't have the luxury of sitting in monasteries or in caves. We're called upon to live our Zen right here and now. More often than not, we've got to do it in the midst of hectic activity, dance not only to the rhythms of our own immediate situations, but to events in the fast-changing world around us. We've got to dance to other people's rhythms too. There's a great opportunity for practice here—especially when those rhythms clash and everything seems to be going haywire.

The old Chinese Zen poet Yung-chia says that being mature in Zen is being mature in expression. How do you express your Zen maturity when you're preparing for a houseful of dinner guests, and your contact lens rolls all the way up into your eye, and you can't get it down no matter what you do? What does being a "spiritual" person mean at such a moment? Perhaps just spending ten minutes in front of the bathroom mirror until you finally get the lens out.

Each of us is unique in the way we "dance." Some are laid-back and easygoing; some are quick and impatient. Others are broad and spacious in their movements, while still others are compact and economical. All of these are perfect as they are. Think of Gene Kelly, Fred Astaire, and Twyla Tharp—all very different kinds of dancers, all brilliant and a delight to watch. There's no one way of dancing. Just because you're easygoing doesn't mean that your rhythm is any more "spiritual" than that of the high-strung person on the cushion next to you. Zen maturity isn't reflected in your disposition so much as it is in how you deal with situations where the rhythm of your life grows chaotic. It's so easy to be tripped up by the rhythm of events that seem to be happening to you, flung at you from somewhere outside. You've just established a nice, comfortable rhythm for yourself and—BANG!—you're knocked off course. It's like the "fundamental koan" established by the great twentieth-century Japanese lay Zen teacher Shin'ichi Hisamatsu: "Nothing you do will do. Now what will you do?"

You either dance as the new rhythmic pattern of each moment, or you get hurt. This means you've got to be so concentrated, so attentive to the moment, that you no longer distinguish between your own personal rhythms and those of the people around you. You open yourself up to the unexpected. And when you don't label the moment, it loses its threat. Still, in order for this to happen, you must lose yourself in the moment. It's hard enough to do on your Zen cushions, when the rhythms of your breath and mind are flowing harmoniously. But it's still harder when rhythms clash, say, when you and your partner are struggling over who is going to lead and who is going to follow.

FINDING THE RHYTHM OF YOUR LIFE

A good place in which to locate the rhythm of your life is your body. Those of us who have worked out around other people in a gym know exactly what this entails. A case in point: we like to work out together. We've developed a program that suits us both. It consists of the treadmill, the stationary bicycle, and a few weight machines. We've divided up our time so that one of us is on the treadmill while the other is on the bike, and so on. Except when it comes to being on time, we find little difficulty adjusting to each other's very different rhythms. Manfred likes to do his routine for no longer than an hour; Perle likes to spread hers out for well over an hour. Usually, our rhythms clash only when we've got someplace to go or something to do together afterward. That's when Manfred seems to be "rushing" and Perle seems to be "dawdling." We used to drive ourselves crazy trying to change each other's workout rhythms until one day we discovered that it wasn't necessary to change anything, only to stop arranging joint appointments before or after working out! The solution was so simple, we almost missed it. We wasted a lot of energy in struggling—first in trying to force each other to change, and when that didn't work, in trying to accommodate to each other. It was only when we stopped trying to do anything at all and just experienced every work-out anew that we discovered the harmony in our clashing rhythms. Now when we're thrust into situations that seem impossibly daunting, we often find the best opportunities for "moving alone together." But it only works when we stop being self-conscious and allow ourselves to dance with the moment.

So, what do you do when the easy, smooth breathing established in zazen gives way to the unexpected intrusion of an accident or an illness? What happens when a familiar situation suddenly turns unfamiliar? Do you live in constant anticipation of disaster? Do you become neurotically obsessive about the weather, for example, when (like us) you live in "Tornado Alley?" Or do you find the opportunity to really practice your Zen by becoming one with the rhythm of your situation no matter what it might be?

As soon as the mind is challenged by an unexpected turn of events, it will go into a tailspin. It's like a monkey, habituated to only one way of doing things and hating to be thrown off course by something new. This "monkey-mind" instantly grows resentful, takes everything as a personal affront: "How could this be intruding on me?" "Here's a new situation. I don't like new situations I didn't create myself." "I hate disruptions that force me to alter the rhythms of my carefully-choreographed daily dance." Whether it's an accident or an illness, or rejection by someone you counted on, or a nasty e-mail message coming at you first thing in the morning at work, or a phone call from school announcing that your child has a reading disability, these are the haywire rhythms that call for maturity in Zen where it counts—not on a mountaintop but right here, responding with the appropriate action. As reflexive and rhythmic as the breath, it can take any number of forms: swerving the car into a ditch to avoid a head-on collision, leaping to avoid that in-line skater rolling right onto the jogging track in front of you, or negotiating your rebellious twelve-year-old's allowance.

In order to find the rhythm of your life, you've got to close the gap between yourself and everything you do—not by following the steps in your head, but by *dancing* it with your entire bodymind. Zen doesn't distinguish between the physical and the spiritual. It doesn't claim that an enlightened person isn't going to have a black-and-blue mark on her shin after falling down on the ice. Yet at the same time, zazen does reveal the busy monkey-mind to be an unreliable arbiter of reality. It also proves that meditative absorption isn't exclusive to the cushions and that we've got to keep practicing in order to become better dharma dancers, more adept at improvising. When we're not making distinctions between strange rhythms and familiar ones, we're less likely to be thrown off by abrupt changes. Most important, we've got to leap into the moment—whatever it has in store for us—if we really want to dance.

JUST KILLING TIME

SPIRITUAL STALENESS

After a few years of Zen practice, we sometimes feel staleness creeping in. Our minds are "captured" by an insidious undergrowth that leaves us "begging for water." We've given our practice so much time and effort, and now, just as we're managing to incorporate that twenty-five minutes of daily zazen into our busy lives, we discover that we've lost the enthusiasm that brought us to sitting in the first place. We take to the cushion regularly, but we aren't really concentrating. Our intentions are fine, but somehow we never manage to separate ourselves mentally from our busy lives. We're so used to accumulating one chore after the next that meditation itself becomes part of that list of chores. We get up in the morning and immediately fall into a robotic pattern so that we can get through our routine tasks. We stop paying attention. We aren't really sharp. We perform one chore in order to move on to the next. We finish the next one in order to move on to the next, and so on. Before we know it, the day's over, an accumulation of chores ready to be stored and forgotten. We're just killing time.

Why do we get diverted by such hypnotic, boring stuff? Why don't we find the moment interesting in itself? Say you're doing nothing but sitting on your cushion, breathing. You're not engaging in some activity, some interesting ritual designed to bring about an elevated state of consciousness. Just sitting and being right there in the moment feels too stark, too uneventful. It can even be painful, as when we call something "painfully boring." Where does boredom leave off and pain begin? Some people might liken it to being in the dentist's chair. Sitting for twenty-five minutes can be boring. It can also be physically painful. In zazen, there's no dentist's music to divert you from the soreness in your knees, for example. Yet, like the dentist's chair, it offers a perfect opportunity for understanding the impulse to close the mind to any experience that isn't "pleasing."

It's a very sneaky, artful dodger, this mind. It can appear to be so innocently intelligent or emotionally sensitive, so probing. One of the things that it always does, regardless of how it works its deception, is try to take you away from the moment. And it always seems to work overtime during zazen. Like that incessant talker sitting behind you at the movies, it totally diverts your attention from the main attraction and puts you at the mercy of a boring, ongoing narrative. Isn't it odd that we get so angry at that talker at the movies and yet let him have full sway over our zazen? We'll do anything to escape the boredom.

Instead of sitting, we read about old Chinese Zen masters tweaking each other's noses and throwing snowballs. It's so much more interesting. Why not vicariously partake of the entertaining stories of the masters when your own practice feels so stale?

THE SHARPEST SWORD

Paradoxically, zazen itself is the only way to cut into that staleness. Zazen sharpens the sword of attention and brings us back
to the moment, which is never stale. Whether appearing as the
evening breeze coming through the window or the backfiring
of a truck, each moment provides the spark that "lights your
dharma candle," as old master Wu-men puts it. No occasion is
too great or too small, and zazen encompasses them all.

There's a koan that shows us the way in the form of a simple question: "What is the sharpest sword?" We try to keep this
koan with us at all times. Right now, for example, where is that
sharp sword? Reading these words, where is it? Turning off the
light, where is it? Fluffing your pillow, where is it? Coughing,
where is it? We ought never let go of that sharp sword—that is,
unless we're to remain satisfied with an existence that simply
drives us or one in which the twenty-four hours rule us. We
can't let sitting become just one more chore, quickly getting
our twenty-five minutes over with and then moving on, finish-
ing our task, our zazen chore for the day. We must see this one
period as a wonderful opportunity, a world filled with the
potential of *being*, for its own sake.

NO GOAL AND NOTHING TO ACHIEVE

Take that twenty-five minutes of zazen to simply let yourself
bask in the delight of breathing. Allow yourself that heart-stop-
ping moment of experiencing a peaceful mind. Just sit down
and, in the first few moments of your meditation, simply count
your breath. Let everything drop away. Consciously dive into
that well of vast space. One . . . two . . . three. There's nothing
you need to know, nothing you need to accomplish. There's
nowhere to go, nothing to hold onto. In those twenty-five

spacious minutes, neither means and ends nor rationality apply. You don't separate, you don't differentiate, you don't conceptualize. You simply flow forth like a mighty stream. One . . . two . . . three. And then, you just stop counting and let the breath itself be your vehicle. The breath itself becomes the whole universe, everything that exists. Unfolding naturally, breathing leads you into that vast and boundless space. You forget yourself, and by forgetting yourself, you awaken to the moment. Or, rather, the moment awakens to itself. For there is no one who awakens and nothing to awaken to. Awakening is just now. Just the sound of the car going by outside, just the clock ticking, just the fragrance of the incense. It's a oneness, an intimacy, an immediacy that is its own purpose, goal, and objective.

We can't emphasize strongly enough how important it is to let go of the goal-oriented, objectivist way of thinking, the state of mind in which you do something in order to get things done. Living like this, you remove yourself from the moment, which has no goal and nothing to achieve. Really, the moment has nothing to achieve! Yet at the same time, as the moment manifests itself, everything is achieved. Achievement occurs; it simply happens. The breath is achievement. Warmth is achievement. Sound is achievement. Just things unfolding, that's how we sharpen the sword. That's how we make of our zazen what the Buddha called a "skillful means" for realizing the moment, our original minds, and ourselves—which, of course, are all one and the same.

COMING TO A COMPLETE STOP

Our former teacher Robert Aitken used to describe zazen as "coming to a complete stop." This is so important, because if we don't stop, we're doomed to wander around in our world of distinctions pulverizing every experience into little pieces.

In this distinction-making world where everything becomes a chore, we live by knowing rather than by being. We're always on the move but never actually arriving. The distinction-making world is important, but it needs to be complemented by the purposelessness of the clock just ticking for its own sake or the breath inhaling and exhaling according to its own rhythm. We need to put these two worlds together. But we can only do this if we work at being in the moment, which is what zazen is all about. There is no need to worry about the world of chores; we know it only too well.

Don't let zazen deteriorate into a chore. Don't objectify it by putting it on your checklist of things to do. Treasure your zazen. Make it a celebration of returning to the one moment. See it as a catalyst that helps you bring the same freshness to all the other activities in your daily life. Sharpen your sword and let it shine. Sharpen the moment and enjoy its radiance. Don't let this opportunity pass you by. Don't be contented simply to drift. Don't cheat yourself of the "real thing"—the fascinating, living experience of the moment—by trading it in for a dry, stale, secondhand life. Don't waste your precious twenty-five minutes of zazen. Let every moment on your cushion be the glorious manifestation of the *Tathagata*.

HARD TIMES, BIG CHANGES

THE FACE OF LOSS

Until we are hit by big changes, we don't usually notice how life and we ourselves are changing from moment to moment. Especially in the face of loss, even people who've been meditating for years find themselves thrust into a new relationship with time. We realized this after a conversation with a friend who had suffered a traumatic change in her life when a tornado swept away not only the physical environment that was so dear to her—the house, garden, trees, and lake where she'd grown up—but also her sense of herself as an artist. She said she felt that her entire identity had been "uprooted."

Listening to her brought tears to our eyes, not because the house couldn't be rebuilt and the trees replanted, but because of our shared human attachment to those things we all hold dear. What does it mean, for example, when we speak of returning to our "true home in the moment" in the face of such disaster? What does it feel like to be smashed to smithereens by change?

Let's look at this on a less monumental scale. We all have

personal "treasures" that we're loathe to part with, such as that pair of shoes we don't have the heart to throw away even though they're falling apart. They feel so good that they become extensions of the relaxed, happy self we like best. Our neighbor, for example, had a pair of sandals he loved. He wore them every day. Then, the very day he came back from a trip and left his sandals out on the porch, they were stolen. He joked about it, but his sense of loss was evident even as he laughed. There's no comparison between having your sandals stolen and losing your childhood home in a tornado, of course, but both involve the feeling of having somehow been personally violated by change. It's this feeling that we have to deal with when our sense of self, our "shrine," has been "ruined."

Do we allow our personal crises to become so all-encompassing that there's no longer any time for zazen? You could argue that it makes good sense to cut back on your usual activities in the face of hard times, particularly when they involve big life changes like unemployment, divorce, illness, or the death of a loved one. It's understandable that we need all our energy to deal with the pain and loss brought about by such events. We don't want to be "diverted" by other activities. It seems natural to say, "I don't want to be bothered by this right now. I have really serious problems to cope with; I have to focus on them." This seems like a natural response, but it's really a strategy for increasing pain and suffering. Why? What is it that we're doing?

ZEN AND PERSONAL CRISIS

When we say, "There's a problem in my life, so I don't have time for practice," we are separating ourselves from our practice, turning it into an object "out there." In fact, we're objectifying both our practice *and* our problem. "I am getting divorced," for example, becomes a thing outside, opposed to the self. Zazen, too, is just another external, disconnected object at loggerheads with our sense of self. By separating or disconnecting ourselves from this thing called "divorce" and this thing called "Zen practice," we're actually increasing the pain that's already been brought about by the divorce. We can't really deal with our situation because we don't enter it fully. By externalizing it, we don't truly become one with what's going on right now, so we're always a step too late. We start thinking in endless circles, mulling over our crisis, trying to tackle it, as if it were an obstacle blocking our path. Because we're spending so much energy wrestling with it, we have no time for other "external objects," such as Zen practice.

This happens when we haven't yet become truly intimate with Zen; we haven't understood, down to our very bones, that it isn't incidental to our lives. We don't see that—like shopping for groceries, fixing the car, buying a new home or losing the old one—our personal crises are not external things. They are instead the very context of our Zen practice; in fact, they *are* our Zen practice. They're all little threads in the gigantic web of grassroots we call our life, which is beautifully revealed in the act of sitting.

Try the following when you are experiencing an intense moment of crisis. Simply focus on your breath as you inhale and exhale, and you'll find that what you thought of as the external, solid form of your crisis isn't solid at all. You'll see that it's not a rock in the middle of the road but a fluid, changing, transitory event. Let the breath show you that the pain you experience as a response to your crisis is not absolute but relative; it is part of a vast web of interdependence that consists of breathing, sitting, talking, walking, and, yes, feeling pain. Let the breath reveal the skein of interwoven moments that make up your karmic tapestry, the patterns of experience, the likes and dislikes. You'll find out soon enough that Zen is not an extra-curricular, fair-weather practice.

Grassroots Zen—ordinary life—has no external referent, nothing outside of itself. This is especially true during moments of personal crisis, when we most need zazen in order to enter the moment.

ONE FOOT IN FRONT OF THE OTHER

Chinese painting is famous for its natural landscapes. Mountains, valleys, and rivers often take up most of the canvas. But sometimes there's a tiny wandering sage in straw sandals carrying a backpack, trudging gaily from the peaks to the valleys, from the riverbanks to the mountains. At times he's clearly having difficulty climbing. At other times, he's taking it easy, sitting on a raft and floating down the river. In some paintings, it's raining and in others, the sun is shining. Yet, regardless of the external circumstances (context) the wandering sage always continues his journey. Although they're always changing, circumstances and journey are really one.

We have to be like that wandering sage, allowing ourselves to feel the pain and exertion that comes with climbing the mountain, and not stopping with the excuse that it's too painful to continue. Putting one foot in front of the other and moving on is the same as paying attention to one breath after the next. That's zazen. That's our practice. Personal crisis is Zen. Zen is personal crisis. Always transforming, personal crisis is just one context in the ever-changing picture of life's patterns. Only by fully entering into the picture, by knowing that the context is always a plurality of things, are we able to let go and see that change. Only then are we able to transform ourselves and our crises. It's essential to keep on walking, never to stop practicing.

If we are to open fully to the event that has become the context of our practice, instead of using a crisis as an excuse not to sit, we need to pay attention to the moment and to the breath—now more than ever.

There is nothing we can do to the "external environment." Transformation comes by itself. We just have to allow it to happen. This doesn't mean being passive or fatalistic about things. Rather, it's being watchful, careful not to slip into the abyss of despair. On the other hand, we may think we're being "spiritual" or "detached" by refusing to identify ourselves with the hard times. But we're really fooling ourselves. That's just another way of closing off to the context.

What emerged from our conversations with our friend who'd lost her home to the tornado was no false detachment, but a basic centeredness, the refusal to be dragged around by the event. It was a mark of her commitment to her Zen practice. In the middle of her troubles, she knew that her true home could never be destroyed. Six months later, she called to tell us that she and her husband and sons were planting new trees on the property around the lake. "It's amazing how the grass has grown back even thicker and greener than before," she said. Then, after a slight pause, she added, "After all these years of painting, I feel I've finally come to understand what 'green' is."

TRUSTING THE MOMENT

SEEING FOR THE FIRST TIME

While Grassroots Zen has no "goal," it is true that the practice has its rewards.

It's just that these aren't immediately visible. They don't show up after a couple of weeks or months of sitting, but only gradually. Sometimes it takes years. It's as though a fog is slowly lifting, allowing us to see more clearly the contours of rivers and mountains, houses, animals, trees, and people. After decades of zazen, we awaken to the "tarnished gold-foil and green leaves" for the first time.

Too often the word "Zen" still conjures up images of stone-faced men in black sitting unmoved in a void. The house blows down around them, but, "So what? We'll build another one. Everything is transient anyway." Someone dear to them dies, and it's, "Oh, that's life and death. It doesn't concern me." Stricken by illness, they wave it off with, "That's the natural way of things. Why should I be disturbed by it?"

This is living death; it has nothing to do with our human, "grassroots" existence. If this were Zen, we'd be the first to run from it.

GRASSROOTS EQUANIMITY

Although it's come up a few times in these pages, "equanimity" is a word we don't use very often. We prefer to speak of trust. "Grassroots equanimity" is a fundamental trust in everything the *Tathagata* brings forth: all the events and, most important, all the moments that make up our daily lives. We can't emphasize enough how important it is to trust the moment if we are to change our anxiety-ridden relationship to time. We must start by tearing down the wall that our conceptual minds erect between ourselves and the moment. It's about eliminating divisions and experiencing interdependence: simultaneously changing, and being changed by, the moment. To enter into such an intimate relationship with the moment, we need unconditional trust. We need to trust life itself. Again, we don't mean naively accepting external events as they unfold. Not at all. We're saying that we've got to trust the fact that our identity, what we think of as a static "self," is actually a dynamic event that is always changing.

Breath is the vehicle of our existence, and it is the only means for developing fundamental trust in the moment. When we sit on our cushions and simply drift, let ourselves be swept away by the past or the future, that's not trusting the moment. It's the opposite of equanimity. Trusting the moment means trusting the breath, melting into it. By losing ourselves in each breath-moment, we set up a boundless mutual flow. We trust the breath and the breath trusts us. Every breath we give is returned, fulfilling us completely. There's nothing more we need; goal and purpose become one. At that moment, our breathing fully expresses everything that exists. The whole universe is part of the process, literally.

When breath and moment merge, there's no one standing outside commenting, "Well, is the whole universe breathing now?" That narrator, too, trusts the breath enough to let go of his privileged position. Nothing, and no one, remains outside. It's what the Japanese Zen master Dogen meant by "a green mountain walking." Not a person taking a walk, but the whole universe walking.

When we really trust in the moment, carried by our breath as lightly as cloud vapor, our minds can finally stop and rest. This is not the petrified, frozen rest of the living dead, but the dynamic, living ease of inhaling and exhaling, expanding and contracting. There's no end to the changing flow. We ride it, like the carefree boy riding the ox in the famous Zen ox-herding pictures. That's equanimity, that's trust. Simple enough? Maybe during zazen, but not so often in daily life. We're riding along smoothly, and circumstances change suddenly. A red flag appears, the ox goes wild, and we're dragged along, clinging to its horns for dear life. It is then that we must learn to trust even the moments we dislike.

TRUSTING MOMENTS WE DISLIKE

Sometimes in the middle of a frenzied day at work we find ourselves looking forward to an evening of zazen. We actually long for the moment when we can finally sit on our cushions and drop everything. No sooner are we nicely arranged, however, than we're beset by thoughts. Our crazy day has followed us into the zendo, and no amount of breath counting can chase it away. The thoughts are too strong, and we can't relax. We can't seem to generate enough effort to let them go; our thoughts are so powerful that they overwhelm any little trust in the moment we can muster. Yet it's precisely because we dislike them so intensely that such jarring moments offer the best opportunities for cultivating trust. Because there's no place to go, nothing we can do to escape them, we simply sit and breathe as those frenzied thoughts. By trusting the frenzied-thought-moment, we recognize that there's no distinction between "me" and "it." There isn't anyone *having* frenzied thoughts, there are only frenzied-thought-moments popping off like firecrackers. Zazen affords us the trust to fully enter those moments, whether they please us our not.

Let's assume you're planning an intimate, candlelight supper to celebrate your husband's birthday. You're just walking out of the door of your office when your secretary tells you that your boss is calling. Taking the call, you learn there's a problem in a computer program that only you know how to deal with, and you've got to stay on for at least another three hours. So much for your husband's birthday dinner.

What do you do now? Just because you practice Zen doesn't mean you won't be disappointed or even feel terrible. The point is to let that wave of disappointment go right through you, acknowledge it, be there with it, become one with it. It's important to acknowledge it.

Very often, we don't acknowledge our disappointments and instead choose to gnaw on them for hours, days, weeks, however long. It's best to acknowledge them right away, and then move on. So, you call your husband and explain the situation; you trust the moment by dealing with it. You become one with that phone call, open to the interaction, to your husband's disappointment, and you turn back to the computer and trust *that* moment as well. You don't separate yourself from the next three hours of work because you want to be somewhere else. You don't spend the next three hours cursing your boss. You take care of the matter at hand, completely and fully, with all your attention, and then you move on. You trust the moments of correcting the hitch, of putting together the list of clients you'll have to call, of standing up and stretching every so often.

By acknowledging your disappointment as it arises, you are trusting the moment; but when that moment comes to an end, you don't refuel it again and again, you simply trust the next moment as it arises, and so you go, gliding through the moments you dislike.

LINKING UP WITH LIFE

Contrary to what most of us are led to believe, equanimity includes the ability to express anger when it's there—but without violence. We have to express the truth of an angry moment with the same honesty we lavish on a moment of love; otherwise we won't be able to focus on solving problems as they arise. As Grassroots Zen practitioners, we seek to experience and express the truth of all moments. To play with a cat, tell our child a story, make love to our partner, play our favorite piece of music, feel the cold of a November morning on our skin, express "green" on the canvas—all of these are true expressions of Zen equanimity. They show how we establish an intimate relationship with the moment. Inevitably, this give-and-take leads to a genuine experience of interdependence.

When our identity is no longer separate from that of the moment, we link up with all those moments we call "life." We don't have to turn ourselves into gods or to detach ourselves from what it is to be human. But remaining aloof from the moment and trying to manipulate it isn't being human either. This is what's called suffering. It stands directly opposed to the interconnectedness of things. Every great spiritual tradition tells us that there is a way out of suffering, and that it has something to do with fundamentally reconsidering our human existence. They all stress the need for a transformation from egotism to selflessness, which doesn't mean totally relinquishing individuality. It means the full realization of the individual in the act of uniting with everything else. It's a transformation in that the self opens up and, in reconnecting to a vibrant whole, becomes one with the entire universe. All it takes is trust in the moment.

BEYOND TIME

BECOMING TIMELESS

These days, with all the talk of genetically engineered human beings, people often ask us if we think zazen will become obsolete. Why would a perfect, computer-driven android feel the need to awaken to a world where "earth has vanished leaving only sky"? We answer by referring them back to the moment. Right now, we're still made of flesh and blood, still vowed to end suffering, and still committed to the Buddha Way. Nevertheless, changing conditions necessitate an ongoing examination of that commitment. Particularly in the West at the beginning of the twenty-first century, what makes Grassroots Zen practice, grounded as it is in ancient Chinese Buddhism, timeless?

PRACTICING THE BUDDHA WAY

We start with the Buddha. Granted, ours is an unorthodox interpretation of the "Buddha Way." It's inspired by Western democratic principles. It's practiced by laypeople with no monastic experience, and, religiously speaking, it isn't even really Buddhist. We don't take "refuge in the Buddha" as the founder of Buddhism or as a figure of salvation. Despite the Buddha's warning to his students, that's exactly what happened in India after he died. His disciples turned him into a god, and today most Asian Buddhists pray to him in the same way Westerners pray to their god. They take refuge in him as a higher power; they don't believe in their own ability to become Buddhas themselves—that is, to meditate and find salvation on their own, as the Buddha instructed.

In many Asian Buddhist countries, laypeople see doing good deeds as their sole religious duty. They support monasteries, temples, and clergy in order to gain merit. They do this so that in some future life they will be reincarnated as monks, since they believe it's important to take a man's body in order to become enlightened. This is a religious letting go of the self, allowing the Buddha and those who make a profession of the religious life to do the spiritual work for them. In return, these good laypeople support the monks. After they have gone through enough reincarnations as householders, they hope they will have earned the right to practice the Buddha Way. Until then, they consider their "practice" to be attending services, praying, supporting religious professionals, and performing religious rituals.

Living in Hawai'i, we discovered how different our American Zen Buddhist practice was from that of the Asian-Americans who had been born into Buddhism, instead of acquiring it, as we did. We're good friends with a very special Vietnamese Zen monk, Reverend Thich Thong Hai, the abbot of a temple on a lovely mountainside in Honolulu, and we always go up to visit him when we're there. When we were first invited to his temple, we expected to be sitting zazen and maybe doing some

chanting. Afterward, we knew there would be a traditional vegetarian Vietnamese community lunch. It was a surprise to find
that there was no meditation, that even Reverend Hai's two
young attendant monks were too busy performing a variety of
rituals to sit, and that Reverend Hai himself led a lengthy service and delivered a Sunday sermon, just like all the other clergy
in the Honolulu churches. The temple was largely given over
to serving a sizable Vietnamese lay congregation with no meditation experience. So, after the service, we and Reverend Hai
and his two monks went into the Buddha Hall, lit incense, and
sat zazen for ten minutes before joining the others in the din-
ing room for a scrumptious vegetarian feast.

In talking to Reverend Hai, we discovered that the congregation did not expect to be led in meditation, that his duties
had less to do with the Zen practice he'd been performing since
he'd been ordained at the age of five, and more with providing
community service. In this, he has been remarkably successful.
As a "boat person" who came to Hawai'i with nothing, he
established a job training and health care center for newly
arrived immigrants, and he recently had managed to create a
Vietnamese Buddhist school for children and a nursing home
for the elderly. When asked who did zazen, Reverend Hai
smiled and said, "Mostly Westerners, people like you two, and
an occasional Western Buddhist monk passing through on the
way back to the Mainland from Asia." He wasn't being sarcas-
tic. In fact, he was pleased that the Zen practice he'd been
taught in the monastery in Vietnam was being carried on by
Western laypeople.

Traditional Asian Buddhism is very similar to our own
Judeo-Christian style of worship. The religious community,
composed of laypeople, gathers in a temple to celebrate holi-
days, births, and marriages, and to commemorate the dead. No
different from what we grew up with. So, what does all this

have to do with experiencing the Buddha Way? What's so timeless about this practice? Two minutes of silence is all you'll get on a Sunday in any Buddhist temple. It's pretty much the same as the two minutes of "meditation" you'll find in any church or synagogue. Is this what we mean by Grassroots Zen?

Even if we shear away all the Asian symbols and rituals, we can't deny that Zen is a meditation practice rooted in Buddhist spirituality. Everything about it points to the Buddha's experience of the true nature of the self. Therefore, the essence of Grassroots Zen is zazen. If we enjoy performing Buddhist rituals, that's fine. But it's our daily commitment to sitting on our cushions that really counts. It's taking our place as the Buddha sitting in meditation under the Bodhi tree, looking up and seeing the morning star and awakening to our true nature. This is the "grassroots" way of taking refuge in the Buddha. It's commiting ourselves to awakening in this very body, knowing ourselves as Buddha, bearing our own salvation. Ours is not a religious practice in the traditional sense. Rather than worship the Buddha, we continue his practice of awakening to every moment—whether formally, on our cushions, at work, or at home. In every facet of our lives, we are taking refuge in the Buddha.

BE A LAMP UNTO YOURSELF

The practice of zazen in time is itself timeless. Why? Because it isn't aimed at gaining anything, it doesn't chart the number of hours, years, good deeds, lifetimes it takes to gain Buddhahood. We only need to be awake no matter where we are or what we're doing, as committed as the Buddha himself to breathing, eating, talking, sitting, feeling, loving. The Buddha never asked anyone to believe in his experience. He advised his students to "be a lamp unto yourselves." Don't follow, don't take anyone's word for it. Don't let anyone be your savior. It's difficult for people to assume this responsibility. It's so much easier to live vicariously through great religious teachers—especially when, given the distance of time and culture, we put them on a pedestal. It's so much easier to take refuge in someone else's experience. We human beings are oddly parasitical that way. Yet, we are told by the Buddha to be our own authority, to stand on our own two feet. We've got to have the courage to take a leap out of time, to plunge into the practice with no guarantees other than our own determination to walk the Buddha Way. It takes guts to strip yourself of all your concepts, notions, rituals. It's very stark, this practice of "nothing special." Maybe that's why so many people would rather read about it than do it. They're attracted by the "Zen aesthetic," only to find when they actually do sit down on the cushions that there are no "aesthetic" experiences, only sore knees and a merry-go-round of thoughts.

Becoming a lamp unto yourself means melting into the changing moment. It's sharing the very same experience that the Buddha is having at this very moment on this very same cushion. There are no distinctions between you and Buddha. That's why, unlike the more traditional Buddhist sects, Zen advises us to "kill" the Buddha when we meet him. What we're killing is the *idea* of the Buddha that keeps us from being Buddha. How do we do this? Only zazen will point us in the right direction. Once we sit down, all goals fade. Time becomes timeless. Peace of mind emerges all by itself.

space

WRONG VIEWS

THE THREE "POISONS"

Locating the self in space is about making a home in the universe. In daily life, it begins with staking out a place in every direction. Like time, space too is temporary, and our little patch of ground is always changing. So what happens when we find ourselves in a space we don't like, where there's something "wrong" with the view? Do we give in to the "poisons" of greed, hatred, and ignorance and let the self run wild?

The Buddha taught that all life is an expression of suffering; everything that exists is in a state of flux, a condition of becoming brought about by *trshna,* which is variously translated as "thirst," "clinging," or "desire." Because of desire, there is coming into existence. Because of coming into existence, there is suffering. The central message of Buddhism is that the end to suffering lies in the "cessation" of desire. As Buddhism moved to China, Tibet, Vietnam, Korea, and Japan, it left behind its original Indian *Theravada* model and became known as *Mahayana*, or in the case of Tibet, *Vajrayana*.

The big difference between the original Theravada Buddhism and its Mahayana offshoot is that in the latter, there are certain forms of desire and attachment that are never given up. One of these is the desire to save the many beings of the world, declared in the Bodhisattva Vow that we chant after sitting zazen. Because there is no end to the practice of saving the many beings, there is no "cessation," no nirvana. Thus, by keeping "thirst" alive, Mahayana Buddhists never completely experience an end of becoming.

GREED

For Grassroots Zen practitioners, it's important to understand that "thirst" also relates to greed for experiences, which bring about suffering. This is not the kind of attachment that we, as practicing bodhisattvas, want to maintain. There is a fundamental difference, however, between greed and "right" desire, or what we call "healthy attachment." To start with, greed always aims at aggrandizing or expanding the self at the expense of everything and everyone else. The image we like to use is that of a grass root growing wild, choking off all the other varieties of life in the field. Healthy attachment, on the other hand, is aimed at showing compassion, considering others, and making room for them to grow.

Confronting greed is essential to Grassroots Zen practice. From the very first breath we take after the bell rings marking the opening period of zazen, we study the way greed arises. It's part of the process of looking into the wondrous workings of the self. We experience on our cushions how ceaselessly the mind moves; how easily it gets diverted; how it loves accumulating and rehashing concepts, ideas, memories, fantasies. That's probably the most basic form of greed—latching onto our favorite ideas and objectives, refusing to let go until they rigidify. Before we know it, they're no longer ideas but cravings we long to fulfill. This is what we mean by aggrandizing or expanding the self.

Greed for money is perhaps the biggest preoccupation in our grassy field of practice. It usually begins with a sincere wish for a salary raise. Harmless enough. But instead of stopping there, the mind spins a story. "What could I get if I were in a different profession or, better yet, if I'd been born into a rich family?" The thought soon becomes more than just a matter of money. Before we know it, we're caught in a spin cycle of never-ending thoughts generated by our initial desire. We're no longer thinking about money but about situations we like and dislike. Now we're propping up the self, searching for ways to make it immune to change and death. We conjure up pleasures that never pass away, fortunes that never turn into misfortunes. In short, we are mesmerized by greed. As a matter of fact, our whole society is based upon this principle of greed. It's called "consumer confidence," which means the more we buy, the "healthier" the economy. "More is preferred to less" is the economic mantra of our age.

If everything in this interdependent world is pervaded by greed, how are we to get a handle on it? What can we do in the face of such powerful social pressure? Aren't we too inextricably tied to events in the world by the results of our own actions?

For us, the answer lies with the "single blade of grass," the individual sitting on the cushion, breaking the habit of greed by appreciating the so-come, so-gone nature of the breath. The antidote to the poison of greed goes to work when we immerse ourselves in this world without objectives, when we simply enjoy life in the grassy field for its own sake. We use zazen as a trowel in clearing away the weeds so we can grow in the space allotted to us.

As always, the breath is our best teacher. It fills our body as we inhale, yet it leaves without a trace as we exhale. Although nothing remains, there is the constant inhalation and exhalation that sustains our lives as bodhisattvas, Grassroots Zen practitioners, women and men, professionals, laborers, family members. There is always the breath, a steady measure teaching us something very fundamental about greed: namely that we only need to inhale and exhale once to complete each breath. The air we inhale must eventually be exhaled. If we hold onto it, we'll burst. We have to let go in order to live.

We're not advocating getting rid of everything and becoming beggars. All it takes is an honest effort to pay attention to the way individual greed arises, becomes an unconscious habit, and thereby strengthens the mass greed of our society. You'd be surprised how quickly those superfluous goals and attachments weaken or simply vanish under the lens of zazen. Such awareness extends beyond the cushion, affecting our social, political, and economic lives as well. Embodying our Bodhisattva Vow, we learn to limit our desires so that there's enough to go around for all the occupants of planet Earth.

Still, no matter how aware we become, there will be no end to "thirst." Greed, hatred, and ignorance are endlessly rising. But that doesn't stop us from working to root them out. In line with the Mahayana tradition, Grassroots Zen is not about cessation. It's about furthering the right desires. And what makes desires "right" is that they are aimed toward the welfare of the many beings. We don't mean to sound sentimental or moralistic here. The kind of "selflessness" we're talking about is more like playing a reed instrument. The notes come and go with the breath. There's still the desire to play, but there's no need to hold on to one note throughout the entire piece. Granted, we'll always play a false note here and there. But that's okay, because mistakes, too, provide the context for our practice. Imagine running out of greed; what would we ordinary human bodhi-sattvas do?

The second of the three poisons, hatred, is actually an exag-gerated form of greed. Where greed emerges from the self-interested impulse to accumulate more and more, hatred is the ultimate expression of isolation. "I hate _____" (fill in the blank) is not only a statement of aversion, but an attempt to dominate the "other." Hatred is an affirmation of the isolated, alienated self at the expense of everything else. Taking it a step further, hatred is the act of destroying the emerging moment so that the desperately alienated self can run roughshod over everything in its path.

The early Buddhist scriptures describe all emotions as forms of energy that we don't understand so much as feel. Hatred is a very strong, very destructive emotion. It's an energy that's quickly squandered, like a fire that burns fiercely but doesn't warm or shed light. We all know its power. All of us have moments on the cushion where we experience hatred emerg-ing. It usually begins with an unspecified sense of unease. Something doesn't feel right. We can't put our finger on it, but there's definitely a feeling of missing something. That's when our desires are looking for something to latch onto. The poet Otsuji aptly describes this very odd sensation as speaking out loud in a voice we don't recognize as our own. It's almost as if a child in us is yelling, "I hate this! I want that, and I want it now!" It's often hard to pinpoint what that child wants, because as soon as we offer one thing, the child goes right on yelling for something else. This little drama leaves us feeling very unsettled.

Without attributing such "unsettled" feelings to a specific source, the ancient Indian philosophers provide a nice description of it. They say there are three *gunas*, pervasive universal energies, that are responsible for our moods. Whether we wake up feeling sprightly, cranky, or depressed depends on the working of these three energies. Modern Western scientists have put it in terms of cosmic influences, attributing human and animal mood changes to celestial phenomena like sunflares or meteor showers. Both explanations refer to the unspecified universal energies contributing to our mood swings.

Unfortunately, instead of working with feelings of unease, paying attention to their appearance, we immediately express them. "I don't feel very good today because I had to spend hours listening to a boring speaker at a conference last night. I was sitting in the front row and he was looking right at me, so I couldn't get up and leave—especially since my supervisor was sitting right next to me, and he'd invited the speaker. I hate my supervisor." We might not really mean that we hate the supervisor; we might only be expressing a mild form of irritation, but we're still unwilling to accept our discontent for what it is. We'd rather rationalize it, justify and expand it until we finally reach the conclusion that the supervisor is responsible for our discontent. We don't like feeling discontented, so someone has to be at fault.

Sometimes we instantly dislike a person for no reason at all. Maybe it's just a lack of affinity. No problem, we can live with it. But we can't let our isolated, alienated self fuel that mild aversion. We're not saying it's easy. Even at those times when we pay attention to the upsurge of hatred directed at someone, we get caught in its unfolding and can't do anything about it. We seem to be powerless in the face of our hatred. We can even be aware of its negative consequences, can almost predict them, and still we let the annihilation of the "other" grotesquely expand.

Is there really nothing we can do? Are we condemned to spend our lives hating? To a certain extent, we're sorry to say that the answer is "yes." But that doesn't mean we stop carrying out our Bodhisattva Vow. We just keep practicing, cutting away the poisonous weed of hatred and making room for compassion to flower in its place.

Believe it or not, it's possible to use hatred to come back to the moment. You simply stop and break for a few seconds of hatred as you inhale and exhale. You care for the moment that is presenting itself as hatred. Without being swept away by it, you simply pay attention to it, realizing that it, like everything else, is a passing form of energy. Your attention itself will put a stop to the hatred. You won't have to act on it, regretting what you've done a day or two later. If the hatred is too strong and won't go away, then be satisfied with putting it into perspective. See how the energy comes and goes with your inhalation and exhalation. Try this with people you really dislike. Listen to them. Broaden your perspective by seeing where they're coming from. If this is too hard, try it with someone you love, a partner or a child. In the middle of a fight, try changing places with your purple-haired teenager. Stop and see how your sense of righteousness expands as you chew him out. See how easy it is to indulge your own one-sided picture of reality. See how it splits you off from your child and turns your relationship into a contest between "me" and "him."

We're all driven by hatred at one time or another. Yet we are also driven by the possibility of realizing that we are no different from those we hate. We may not be able to get rid of hatred altogether, but we can certainly put limits on how much we let it grow.

For example, we had a particularly hard time dealing with our own hatred-prone inner child when we moved to Illinois and found ourselves living in a university town called "Normal." In addition to its laughable name, Normal stands for everything we're not: it's politically conservative, anti-intellectual, afraid of diversity, and obsessed with property values. Like most booming American small towns, it's made up of endless subdivisions of lookalike houses thrown up overnight by greedy developers. Family farms are being swallowed up by huge, polluting agricultural conglomerates, and prairie land is being paved over by strip malls and shopping centers. An extension of the university campus, the town's main street is two blocks long, and its bars, tattoo and pizza parlors cater mainly to students. It would be unfair not to mention that there are also three excellent gift shops, a fine vegetarian deli-restaurant, a good used-book store, and an art film theater.

We spent a good part of our first year "hating Normal" before coming to see it for what it is: the place where we live, perform meaningful work, have wonderful friends, and a progressive action network that fosters our social responsibilities. Now we're going into our fifth year here, and although we haven't totally settled into *liking* Normal, we can honestly say that—thanks to our Zen practice—we no longer hate it.

IGNORANCE

Ignorance is the foundation of the "three poisons," which are the source of suffering. From a Buddhist perspective, ignorance is not simply the opposite of conceptual "knowing," as in not taking an umbrella because you don't know it's raining. Ignorance is much deeper than not knowing. It actually addresses the way we see ourselves, our environment, and our actions. Being ignorant means not knowing the self, having no understanding of its true nature, no "self-realization." Ignorance is the basis for speaking aloud and not knowing your own voice. It's thinking, "I'm in here and you're out there." It's drawing a sharp line that distinguishes you from others, so you can do whatever you want without worrying about the effects your actions will have on them. The sharp line falsely assures you that there'll be no repercussions.

Whenever ignorance closes our eyes to the interdependent nature of the moment, we suffer. Finding ourselves thwarted, we double our efforts at getting what we like and avoiding what we don't like. We struggle to free ourselves from a trap we can't get out of. Yet the more we struggle, the worse it gets. Exhausted finally, we stop thrashing around and start examining our condition. We start with what's closest: the breath. Instead of seeing our breathing as something "out there," we become one with it. The boundaries between "me" and "my breath" break down. We're still conscious. It's not as if we fall into a trance, but the quality of our consciousness changes. It now includes the breath, the dripping of the faucet, the rustling of the leaves, the barking dog—everything that's going on. Master Dogen calls this "body and mind dropping away." And when this happens, the poisons of greed, hatred, and ignorance drop away as well.

RIGHT VIEWS

CLARITY

When we call someone a "clear thinker," we're usually associating clarity with the mental space of conceptual knowledge. This is the clarity of boundaries, substance, particularity. It's seeing an object as distinct from other objects. This isn't the clarity of Zen. In fact, it's the opposite. The problem for most of us is that we're so habituated to distinguishing among objects "out there," that it's hard to enter a world where there are no distinctions. And this is exactly what Zen demands: entering the world of the moment, of flux, of perpetual unfolding. To be "clear" in Zen is to be one hundred percent part of that unfolding. As soon as we stop and say, "Oh, what was that experience? Where did it come from? In what way is it different from the experience I had yesterday?", we're engaged in a search for analytical clarity. We stop the flux by removing ourselves from it, thereby creating a static object called the "self." It's this onlooker that creates other static objects and no longer wants to flow along with events. This is how we lose clarity, which is understood in Zen terms as "coming and going."

There's always the temptation to make these analytical stops, especially when we sit. When certain emotions or bits of thought drift by, we seize upon one of these and want to clarify it or interpret it. We create a story around it or try to deal with it in a conceptual way. Of course it's impossible to clarify this endless stream of consciousness. Fortunately, there's the breath; whenever we catch ourselves running off with an idea, we can go right back to counting our inhalations and exhalations. We can give the old narrator in our minds something better to do, until, gradually, he steps out of the picture. Once he's gone, once we've let go of the analytical mind and the "clarity" that comes from dividing subject and object, there's room for the clarity of just this one inhalation, just this one exhalation, just this one breath-moment.

UNFOLDING IN THE MOMENT

In Zen poetry, the "harvest moon" is symbolic of the enlightened mind. Sitting at the center of a "shining sky," its clarity is boundless. It pervades the whole universe. It's dynamic without being limited by time or space. It doesn't yield to classification. We can't impose categories on it. Yet it's always "painting silhouettes"—seeing, hearing, smelling, tasting, touching, unfolding by itself—if we let it. Zen clarity is filled with sensory awareness, but it isn't conceptual. Really seeing can't happen when there's a subject in here and an object out there. This is our great challenge, on our cushions and as we go through life.

In the grassy field of our practice, where conceptual thinking is so highly valued, it's particularly hard to let go into the clarity of the unfolding moment. But it's not impossible. Even if we have to engage in conceptual thinking, we can still open ourselves to "just thinking." We can let thinking become no different from hearing or seeing or tasting. The Chinese, for example, call thinking our sixth sense. They don't place it on a pedestal above all the others, the way we do. If we just think "3+4=7," the way we just see "house, window, flower pot," then we can open up to the clarity of thinking for its own sake. It's harder to "just think" in the office than to "just breathe" on our cushions, but it's really worth practicing. It's part of the process of regarding every moment as an opportunity to clarify what our lives are about.

Our Grassroots Zen practice begins when we try to clarify existential questions having to do with change: "Why do I have to grow old?" "Why do I have to die?" By the time we get to the cushion, our minds are exhausted. None of the conceptual answers satisfy us. They never will. That's because our minds are in the habit of "clarifying" by conceptualizing, analyzing, scrutinizing, examining, dissecting, creating distance between ourselves and our questions. The more we engage in this process, the more restless we become. Finally, we hit the wall. We're frustrated and angry when we pick up a Zen book and read that the answer is right there in front of us. Why don't we see it?

Reading isn't enough; we have to sit down and partake of the clarity that's right here in this unfolding moment. We ourselves must pass through old master Wu-men's "gateless gate," the guardless checkpoint through which we are always freely coming and going.

SUDDENLY THE SKY BREAKS OPEN

The analytical mind itself is the obstacle to partaking in the unfolding moment and seeing clearly. If that's the case, then it's the mind that must put itself at ease. We can start by taking a detour around the obstacle of discursive thinking. This is what

the mind does in meditation; it clarifies itself in the act of uniting with the breath. "Suddenly the sky breaks open," says Master Wu-men, "heaven and earth are astonished." Why are they
astonished? Because everything is so clear from the very beginning. Clarity is always there, so there's nothing to clarify. This
sounds like a philosophical conundrum, a verbal trick, but it's
really not. A Zen friend of ours described her experience of
clarity as "so obvious, so simple, that I couldn't stop laughing
when it first hit me. I had to go outside and roll around on the
grass." When the great Chinese Zen master Lin-chi "clarified
the great matter," he said, "Oh, is that all there is to my teacher
Huang-po's dharma?" Lin-chi wasn't downgrading Huang-po's
teaching; he was marveling at the obvious.

As soon as the vista opens, as soon as the wind blows
through us and the birds sing in our voices, we no longer need
to clarify anything. We *are* clarity. "The great way has opened
and there are no obstacles." This is our task as Grassroots Zen
practitioners, to walk that "great way" and to help others clarify it for themselves by reaching out and walking with them
along that dusty road. We have to clarify the matter together, as
a grassroots community, for the process of clarifying is linked to
the experience of interdependence. It's actually the realization
of interdependence. We can't begin to clarify anything without
becoming one with "the world of the red dust," as the Chinese
so poetically put it. This can't be done by withdrawing from the
world but only by embracing it. We must actively partake in the
great cosmic celebration that is always in progress, linking all
beings in the great flow of consciousness.

ERECTING BARRIERS WHERE THERE ARE NONE

There's nothing mysterious about Zen practice, yet we can't
seem to stop complicating things. We think we somehow have

to transcend this mundane world in order to cross into the clear light. When we give a workshop, there's inevitably a question about purification. "Don't we have to purify ourselves, make our minds empty so that we can see clearly?" The question itself is a good example of conceptual thinking. Reading too many "spiritual" books often enlarges our expectations. They tell us about angels, astral walking, stunning states of transcendence, and perfect peace. No wonder so many spiritual seekers think clarity has to be something special. It couldn't happen right here in this very mundane moment. It's got to be out there somewhere. And off they go, from one workshop to the next, hoping to catch "it."

Spirituality itself can be an obstacle to clarity. It's the idea of clarity the mind creates for itself, the one that diverts attention from what's right here now and considers it unworthy. Setting up distinctions between "sacred" and "profane" worlds, we erect the barriers ourselves. Then we get disappointed when we don't have mysterious experiences.

Though it may not sound like much, the greatest experience available to us is becoming one with the moment and realizing that the space we inhabit is already clear and perfect as it is. We've said it many times, but it really is the most satisfying "spiritual experience" we humans can ever have. It's the only one that answers all the questions, clarifies them once and for all. A good example of this is the legend of the seeker who comes to Bodhidharma, the founder of Zen in China, hoping to become his student. It's snowing, and Bodhidharma is sitting zazen in his cave. The man waits outside for three days until finally he gets so desperate, he cuts off his arm. Bodhidharma comes out and asks him, "What do you want?" The man replies that he's looking to put his mind to rest. "Bring me this mind, and I'll put it to rest for you," says Bodhidharma, and instantly, the man is enlightened. That's the mind we've got to work on, but not by cutting off our arm.

We don't have to create waves when the ocean is flat. The effort only comes when we ourselves create those waves. But even then, finding ourselves in the middle of a big wave itself presents us with an opportunity. All we have to do is dive right in.

CONTAINING MULTITUDES

DHARMA RELATIONS, KARMA RELATIONS

Nakagawa Soen Roshi once reflected on the difference between painful karmic relationships and wonderful dharmic connections. Aiming his remarks specifically at a group of Western Zen students, he noted how easily interpersonal problems find their way into "sangha relations." In the East, where Confucian social and cultural norms regulate behavior in Zen communities, interpersonal problems aren't usually aired in public. These norms have been superimposed on Buddhism and are often hard to reconcile with the democratic nonduality of the Buddha Way. Yet Asian Buddhists have somehow managed to balance the hierarchical, Confucian way of life with the cyclical, nondualistic tenets of Buddhism and Taoism from which Zen emerged.

We puzzled over the matter when we found Western Zen groups chanting the traditional invocation to "let true Dharma continue, sangha relations become complete." Why do sangha relations have to become complete? As an integral part of the Dharma, isn't sangha already full and complete as it is? All we have to do is plug into it when we sit, and the Dharma simply reveals itself to us. When we come together and practice as a community, aren't we "practicing" the Dharma? What is "true Dharma" anyway? And why are karmic relations so often in conflict with it?

We find this chant very telling. If sangha relations need completing, it means that there's something still open. There's a break in the circle that somehow has to be joined. Yet if you practice Zen long enough, you come to realize that there is no such thing as completion or perfection. The Zen poet Leonard Cohen describes it as the "crack in everything" that lets the light in. If even the Buddha hasn't finished practicing, the Dharma must be infinite, an open space without closure. There is no final goal of perfection to be reached.

There's another way of looking at "dharma," though. As Krishna tells Prince Arjuna in the great Indian epic, the *Bhagavadgita*, "Your dharma is your duty, your religious, social, and family obligations." In this context, it refers to the laws of daily life. It has to do with practical ethics and moral behavior. Do you behave "dharmically" in your business dealings, in your intimate relationships, in your relationship to the earth and its many beings? It's the practice of right livelihood, of being "dharmically" involved with the community, both in and out of the zendo. These various levels of "dharma" are interestingly nuanced and, depending on the situation, have different meanings.

"Let true Dharma continue and sangha relations become complete" refers to the formal Dharma, within the context of Zen practice. It reiterates the connection not only to the immediate sangha but to all those who came before and will come

in the future. In this sense, "sangha relations" refers to the Buddhist lineage of Dharma practitioners.

Grassroots Zen practitioners have to establish that connection without any formal lineage charts. Because we aren't part
of an official Zen temple and don't have any Buddhist Dharma
successors or ordained priests or nuns or monks among us, we
become a sangha merely by sitting together. Our relationship to
the Dharma is affirmed each time we "entangle eyebrows with
the ancestors" on our cushions. We're grateful to the people
who sowed the seeds so that the Dharma could sprout in us and
come to fruition in a grassy field where "chrysanthemums and
jonquils" can be found "blooming together." With each breath,
we thank the Buddha and Bodhidharma, Lin-chi and Dogen,
as well as the person sitting on the cushion next to us, for linking us to our roots in the "Dharma family."

Why, then, must karmic relations be so horrible? Why are
there so many family problems in this long line of dharma relations? We say it's because karma is part of dharma, part of what
it is to be human.

THERE'S NO AVOIDING CAUSE AND EFFECT

Everyone and everything is bound by karma, the law of cause
and effect. Even enlightened people cannot evade the law of
Karma. Let's say we've been insulted and are feeling anger. We
say the insult has caused us to be angry. When did it change
from being an insult into a feeling of anger? At what moment
did a "dharmic" person turn into a "karmic" one? Can dharma
and karma be teased apart? Is there one without the other? Is
there even a "practice" without human beings, filled with
greed, hatred, and ignorance as we are? Not really. Not if you
don't want to be reborn as a fox. Only human beings embodied in this package of karmic tendencies can sit zazen and

realize "true Dharma." There is no Dharma without karmic relations—good or bad.

It's not peaceful to be a karmically related human being. It's a bit of a miracle that we can make dharmic connections at all; that of all the possible permutations and combinations, we find ourselves among kindred spirits in the grassy field of this world. Still we have to be careful not to set dharma against karma. We mustn't turn Dharma into an ultimate ideal of perfection. Rather than split one perfect set of relationships against another imperfect set of relationships, let's simply tune in to whatever happens to be manifesting in the moment: a smiling face, a frowning face, praise, blame. It's not that they're all the same. That would be a misunderstanding of Zen practice. A slap in the face is certainly different from a kiss. It's better to pay attention to the anger rushing through on the heels of that insult—then let it go.

CULTIVATING A SPACIOUS MIND

When Walt Whitman wrote that he "contained multitudes," he was criticized for being arrogant. His critics didn't know that his assertion came from the experience of meditating every day during his lunch hour. Meditation had made his mind, and his heart, spacious enough to contain the entire universe, even when confronted by the worst that karma had to offer. Because we are unique individuals, we are often difficult to deal with. Add to that our distinct karmic dispositions, temperaments, cultural and genetic inheritances, and you've got plenty of opportunity either to contain multitudes or annihilate them. This is especially true when, like our friend Bill, you're a Zen practitioner and a high-powered businessman. We asked him how he juggles the Zen ethic of "right livelihood" with the demands of his job, and he wrote:

The competitive dynamic of the business world often reminds me less of life in the marketplace than of life in the wild. The "survival of the fittest" instinct in human beings may seem primitive, but it appears to be a reality in our "natural" world as well as in the business world. How does a Zen student like me apply the fruits of meditation in a world that is forever challenging my equanimity? How do I avoid suppressing my desires and instincts and find a way of accepting their authentic expression? Does a balance exist in our lives between such expression and responsible, ethical action? Zen teaches us to engage with and accept the "suchness" of the world "as it is," and it would seem that the same holds true for human nature and life in the business world.

In business, we ride the tides of bias and ethics, all the while trying to maintain efficiency in cost controls and creativity in marketing; ultimately aiming to make a profit or at least survive. In this arena, we find the opportunity of balancing our desires and ambitions with the rhythm of the moment. Each time life knocks us off balance, the mind either resists or, like an Aikido specialist, rolls with the punch and incorporates this rhythm into our next expression ... [I] have addressed these questions in my Zen practice simply by engaging moments of daily living, whether at the office or at home, with the spirit of suchness. And since engaging each and every moment is beyond most of us, I find myself from time to time returning from the rushing whirlwind of my daily life to the present act of closing the car door or walking to my next appointment. Nonetheless, I sometimes return with anger or anxiety caused by the business world's effect on my resisting mind. Life beyond the cloistered walls of ritual and religious formality offers me infinite possibilities for engaging compassionately with the world.

It's easy to denigrate the marketplace and idealize the monastery. But all you have to do is read a little history to see

that even the Buddha and his sangha had their share of competitive clashes. In fact, one of the Buddha's disciples grew so
hostile that he tried to poison the Buddha. Zen history, too, is
full of conflict. In China, the appointment of the sixth ancestor as Dharma successor was so resented that he had to flee the
monastery for his life. According to legend, a mob of monks ran
after him, prepared to kill him. Imagine, Buddhist monks who
devote their entire lives to "the Dharma"—the first law of
which is to do no harm—running after a brother monk with
the intention of killing him! It's no surprise, then, that ordinary grassroots practitioners like us still have trouble embracing other sangha members, not to mention the multitudes.

Clearly, dharma and karma are of a piece, and it's our task,
part of our commitment to Zen practice to learn how to swing
back and forth with their ever-changing play. We must balance
our ideal of sangha harmony with the realities of our fractured,
personality-ridden karma. We have to make a conscious effort
to behave "dharmically," to be considerate of other people's
ideas, refrain from shouting them down when they conflict
with ours.

There's something else at work when we're dharmically
interacting. The more we practice dharma, the more it infuses
our karmic activity. Anyone who has interacted on this level
recognizes having moved beyond the limitations of the self,
opening up to others without immediately spouting forth crit-
ical judgments. When we give in to our karmic tics, we're never
comfortable. We're always annoyed by someone, whether it be
Darrell's voice or Sylvia's way of dressing. However, continued
practice discloses our mysterious connection to these people. In
certain dharmic moments, we may even see them as ourselves.
Jessica, a longtime member of our sangha, describes how sesshin
does this for her: "By the morning of the third day, I find myself
annoyed with everyone in the sangha, picking out the single

traits in each person I dislike most. Seeing this critic come up in me, just being with her, is the best practice. When I'm really doing it well, the critic usually shuts up by supper. By the fourth day, I love them all."

In some sense, our obligations as grassroots practitioners are less formalized than they are for traditional sanghas. So we have to be more sensitive to the Dharma in the karma, the presence of the formless in our world of form. We stand more in danger of losing sight of the Dharma in our daily preoccupations, the overstimulation coming at us from advertising, kids whose only interest in life appears to be skateboarding, jobs that increasingly remove us from our families, let alone our spiritual connection to the Zen community. Our problem isn't so much about floating around in emptiness as it is being suffocated by form. Our minds are increasingly overcrowded; we really have to make an effort to clear them, to provide space for the Dharma to manifest in our karmic activities.

We must learn as we practice, how to walk the fine line between Dharma and karma in our relationships to our grassroots friends, our teachers, our colleagues, families, and, ultimately, to the world of the many beings. That's the only way we'll ever be able to "save" them, as we profess to do in our Bodhisattva Vow. The only way to save people is by embracing them as no other than ourselves. By refusing to be swept away by karmic likes and dislikes and violent emotions, we unite the apparently conflicting Dharma/karma relations, and they become complete. It's tough for individualists like us, but it's the only way to go.

> BOUNDLESS AND FREE IS THE SKY OF SAMADHI.
>
> BRIGHT THE FULL MOON OF WISDOM!
>
> TRULY, IS ANYTHING MISSING NOW?
>
> NIRVANA IS RIGHT HERE, BEFORE OUR EYES;
>
> THIS VERY PLACE IS THE LOTUS LAND;
>
> THIS VERY BODY, THE BUDDHA.
>
> HAKUIN

THIS VERY PLACE

HEAVEN AND EARTH

There are only a few passages in Zen Buddhist writings that sum up the practice in one or two sentences, and the last two lines of Japanese Zen master Hakuin's *Song of Zazen* are truly among the best. They capture the essence of the self as the "root that is no abode."

"This very place is the Lotus Land; / This very body, the Buddha." At first glance, Hakuin's imagery seems odd. Although there are Buddhist sects devoted to finding salvation in paradise, we don't usually associate dualistic images of heaven and earth with Zen. The Lotus Land is best known as the paradise of Pure Land Buddhism, an actual place representing the cessation of suffering. There are no disturbances in this paradise, only perfect peace. Like their Christian and Muslim counterparts in the West, many Buddhists believe in the existence of such a place. But here, in an interesting departure from Buddhist tradition, Zen master Hakuin seems to be claiming that earth itself is paradise, that this very place is heaven. How is that possible? After all, isn't he talking about the world of suffering, of change, of coming and going? This world, our world, is one where, by definition, we're never perfect, never free from suffering. We're never there. And yet, Hakuin seems to suggest that, indeed, this very place is where we find peace. This very place of suffering, of change, is nirvana. The emphasis here is on this *very* place—right now.

THIS VERY PLACE

There are many different ways of talking about a sense of place, so we'll start by defining what it means for the typical Grassroots Zen practitioner. It's our place in the family, the town, and neighborhood in which we live, the place to which we feel especially connected, the one we call "home." Extended beyond the family, it's our place at work, what we do for a living, our office, classroom, studio, lab; and it's our intellectual and cultural place: our newspapers, books, radio, television, film, food, art, sport. All of these form the context of our sense of place. They're what Hakuin is referring to.

Going beyond our conventional definition, however, Hakuin cuts right through to the heart of the matter. "This very place" is not something separate or apart from us. It's the moment where our context and our individual existence intersect, touch, and literally become one. It's the place where we no longer try to put distance between ourselves and other things, people, or places. This very place is where we no longer live in duality. (Here we're talking about the kind of duality that cuts us off, makes us feel distinctly different, set apart.) This very place is the place of zazen. It's where we see and become familiar with "this place" through our breath. It establishes the sense of place that Hakuin talks about. It makes very real for us the fact that this very place is the Lotus Land, the place of peace, right where we are. It refers to the entire context, the intersection of a dark night, a cool house, a floor, a carpet, a chair, two friends in conversation. There really is no space between us, only the idea of space that we ourselves have created.

Once we locate this very place, everything becomes vibrant, interdependent, whole, a community of being. There's no need to go to heaven. Even when we're traveling around in the world—for example, commuting to work or visiting relatives at Thanksgiving—traveling itself is manifesting this very place. We're there with every step we take.

When resting in the moment becomes the very foundation of our lives, we can be busy or relaxed, tired or awake, suffering or blissful, but we'll always be in the Lotus Land. We'll experience all kinds of conditions, but they won't change the fundamental truth that this very condition, the one we're experiencing right now, is paradise. This very moment is the full and complete expression of the universe, of everything that is. And it's through zazen that we literally begin to embody this truth.

THIS VERY BODY

Sitting is physical, empirical, rooted. We need a body in order to sit. So if we have to establish a sense of place, a home in the moment, we also have to establish a sense of body, of physicality. Too often, spiritual people (not excluding Zen practitioners, by the way) have a very troubled relationship with the body. There's the feeling that only ideals are real, and that they're somehow cursed to be wandering around in bodies. Unless they're sick or in pain, or undergo surgery, or grow old and are no longer as spry as they once were, many spiritual people pay little attention to their bodies. In fact, those moments when the body starts demanding attention make it all the more hateful to them. It feels like heavy ballast, a distraction from "real" spiritual practice. Such people see their bodies as adversaries.

A young woman spoke in one of our classes about her struggle with anorexia. Raised in a devout Catholic household, she embarked on a spiritual path early on in life. By the time she reached high school, however, she had concluded that it was impossible to be really spiritual without undergoing purification of the body. She began by fasting several days a week. It wasn't long before she had stopped eating altogether. Soon, except for sprinkling a few drops of water on her lips and tongue, she discontinued drinking as well. By the time she was taken to the hospital, she was almost dead. When asked what motivated her drastic behavior, the young woman replied: "I was certain that I'd never become a truly spiritual person while I was still in a body."

This isn't Zen understanding. Quite the opposite. The body is really our first home, our first sense of place. It allows us to realize our true nature, to manifest the whole universe. It's actually a wonderful instrument, as precious as a Stradivarius violin or a Steinway grand piano. It's our responsibility to keep that instrument tuned. We have to pay attention to it, to care for it in the same way we're being told these days to care for our soul. There's no disconnection between soul and body. Cherishing one means you're cherishing both. We have to keep our bodies healthy and treat the wonderful home we occupy as the true manifestation of the Lotus Land. The body is not something to get rid of in order to practice; it's the very instrument of practice. Without it, there's no realization. That's why disembodied spirits and angels can't awaken. We must deeply appreciate the body because, as Hakuin tells us, it is the Buddha.

The body actualizes the truth of this very place as the Lotus Land. Without the body, there can be no peace and contentment, no Zen practice, no following the wonderful path of the

Buddha Way. Instead of seeing the body as a "necessary evil," we have to develop the proverbial Zen quality of "grandmotherly kindness" toward it and all embodied beings: people, snails, sangha, trees, rivers, the grassy field that is this world—they're all connected, all one body. We have to learn to care deeply for the entire body of the universe, for every last thing in this world of the ten thousand things.

CARING

This very place, this very body is all the paradise we need. There's nothing excluded, nothing too great or too small; everything is worthy of care. Caring is perhaps the most fundamental expression of Zen wisdom. Put another way, it's the refusal to let life become a routinely mechanical sequence of events. It rejects simply getting by, not living up to our human potential. In this careless state, where we're happy to let things slide, we don't pay attention to the moment. We simply let life steer us wherever the winds of change will blow. No doubt there are some instances where operating on "automatic pilot" is necessary, but it certainly can't be the way we live our Grassroots Zen practice. The herd behavior that often passes for enthusiasm is better suited to the distractions of the sports stadium.

It takes effort and dedication to realize that this very place is the Lotus Land and that this very body is the Buddha. This is practical wisdom, not an intellectual understanding of the "symbolism" of Hakuin's poem. By practical wisdom, we mean that it's expressed in our ability to care, open up, and unite with the undercurrent of compassion that enlivens the Lotus Land. We honor this very place by bearing witness to this wonderful mystery we call life.

Caring begins and ends with zazen. Without it, our lives have no fuel, no warmth, and no energy. We need to practice in order to care for the body, for this very place. And because we are living in very uncaring times, it's essential that we practice together. Left to ourselves, it's too easy to slip into the insensibility of our everyday habits and routines, merely going through the motions at work and in our relationships. We're not saying it's possible to maintain a caring attitude all the time; there's always a trade-off between routine and active engagement. But caring is knowing that no matter where we are or what we're doing, nirvana is always right here, before our eyes.

COMING HOME

For us, the quintessential American coming home story is *The Wizard of Oz*. In our Grassroots Zen version, Dorothy's search for the magic land of Oz is the quest for the self, our own "true home." Her friends—the Tin Man, the Scarecrow, and the Cowardly Lion—represent the greed, hatred, and ignorance that blind us to the true nature of the self; Toto, the witches, and the wizard are the teachers who provide the guidance, equipment, and obstacles needed for the journey; and the green city of Oz is the grassy field of our practice. The ruby-red slippers stand for zazen, revealing that we never left home to begin with. Like *The Wizard of Oz*, our story is also about discovering our long-lost home in the least expected place—right here, in the present moment. The only difference is that our story never ends. That's because we have to keep practicing—waking up from our dream—over and over again.

LIVING WITH LIMITATIONS

SPIRITUAL GROWTH AND NARROW SPACES

Strictly speaking, we don't live "with" limitations so much as we live "as" them. It's just that we've gotten into the habit of looking at life from the inside out. When the boss creates a new policy that limits us, we say, "Oh, well, I guess I'll have to live with it, like it or not." It's one way of confronting challenges to our space. Another way is to quit our job. But when we've matured a little in our Zen practice, we come to see that we are no different from the limitations we're experiencing. We see ourselves as limitation, constraint, change, and so forth. Once we've bridged the space between ourselves and the moment, there is no one experiencing some event or condition out there that occupies a different space from the one in here. Experience isn't being thrown at us like a ball. We aren't catching it or throwing it back, nor are we contemplating it. Rather, we are one with the experience itself. As in the case of the "resting snail," there's no telling "which end is which."

To look at it concretely, living as limitation when you have a cold, for example, is living as sniffling, as stuffed up. In this very moment, your life is manifesting as a cold.

Trouble is, we don't usually see it this way. We feel we're being constrained by circumstances, imposed upon by a virus. If we're really physically impaired, the boundaries between us and the freedom to live as we want appear even greater.

SURVIVAL

When we talk of survival, we have to realize that we are living in the relative peace and prosperity of a technologically advanced country. Most Grassroots Zen practitioners are comfortable, middle-class people who don't live under the constraints that fall into the category of survival. We don't have to fear being devoured by tigers. We don't have to worry that the mushrooms we're about to eat may be poisonous; we go to the supermarket and assume that, because they're wrapped in cellophane, they're not. Never mind that their long-range effects may be poisonous because they've been sprayed with pesticides; in the short-run, at least, we can be pretty sure we won't keel over and die at the first bite.

On a day-to-day basis, what we conceive of as limitation is more mental than physical; it's something we build up ourselves. Going from the first level of raw survival to the more immediate level of our everyday lives, it's more realistic to look at the limitations we ourselves read into conditions—what we think of as somehow hampering our will. We might be limited financially or professionally. Our work may not be highly regarded or socially useful. We ourselves may have freely chosen our professions, we may love making art or music, say, but the world around us isn't particularly interested in what we've got to offer. So what do we do? We start measuring ourselves against the world around us. Sometimes, like a woman we knew in graduate school, we become paralyzed by this. Helen was an outstanding student. Her professors expected only the best from her. Yet, after completing her Ph.D. written and oral exams with honors, she could somehow never get herself to start work on her dissertation. Because she always became very defensive whenever anyone brought up the topic, people eventually stopped asking her about it. Years went by before Helen confided to a friend over dinner that she'd been raised in a family of perfectionists, held to impossible writing standards by parents who demanded she "write like Dostoevsky or not bother writing at all." No wonder she never managed to write her dissertation!

DOING THE RIGHT THING

Helen might be an extreme case, but it's very human to make "invidious comparisons," as one of our Zen teachers liked to call them. We wonder why it is that something we find so noble, so important to humankind, is seen as insignificant. This is even more appropriate in the case of Zen practice. Why go into sesshin, for example, when you could easily take that week off and play golf, or when you could take that computer course and hone your skills? Practicing Zen is a limitation we set on ourselves. In very real ways, it sets us apart from the "outside world," especially when we take into account what the outside world considers worthwhile: fun, fame, and fortune. We might tell ourselves, "Yes, I'm doing the right thing. I would choose to practice if I had to do it all over again; but I do feel limited, a little set apart from my family and friends who don't practice."

If we're really serious about it, we have to take a good hard look at Zen and the world we're so worried about—the social situation, time, and place, which are the context of our practice.

Take our early "grassroots" forebears in China, the ts'ao-pen
ch'an practitioners. Living in the feudalistic Sung dynasty, they
were born with limitations we can't even begin to imagine.
The social mobility we take for granted in the United States
today was unheard of then. A businessman had to remain
within his socially determined constraints as a businessman. He
might have been well-to-do, but he could never hope to see his
son marry anyone but another businessman's daughter. He may
have been able to afford it, but he and his family weren't
allowed to wear fine silk clothing, a privilege reserved only for
aristocrats. The lines between a monk and a businessman who
practiced Zen were equally hard and fast. For example, in the
earlier T'ang dynasty, during the so-called "golden age of Zen,"
the moment Layman P'ang decided to become a serious Zen
practitioner but not a monk, he nonetheless had to cut himself
off from his former life and give up everything he owned.
Imagine what it would be like, at the peak of your success, to
have to give it all up—family, property, farm animals, furniture.
Then, accompanied only by your daughter (also a Zen devo-
tee), you would sell bamboo housewares to support yourself
and become a traveling Zen teacher.

There were many lay practitioners like P'ang in ancient
China: artists, poets, scholars, farmers. Given their restricted
social status, we'd say they were doing something unique and
revolutionary. Were they doing the right thing? We think so.
Would we be brave enough to do it? We'd like to think so.
Measured against the world of their times, they were taking
even a bigger chance practicing Zen than those who entered
the religious life. At least monks and nuns had a place to sleep
and two meals a day.

On the other hand, a caste system lends itself very well to
Zen practice, which is fraught with limitations. We're limited by the timekeeper's bell, the cushion space, the range of

movement. There are any number of limitations we impose on ourselves to do this practice, which, socially speaking, is itself limiting in that it sets us apart from what most other people in our society do in their valuable spare time. Like the old Chinese grassroots practitioners, we go to sit when our relatives and friends would rather see us doing something else. Today it's almost inconceivable that someone would give up creature comforts, social status, and community acceptance to wander around as a Zen hobo, living from hand-to-mouth. The only comparison that comes to mind is the Beat poet Jack Kerouac and other "Dharma Bums" of the 1950s. But with a few notable exceptions, they were more about poetry and drugs than about a life dedicated to zazen.

Yet it can't be denied that we experience a strange kind of fulfillment from this limitation. You could even say that we enjoy being "outsiders." Of course, it's not as bad for us as it was for Grassroots Zen practitioners in ancient China. Their world was so hierarchically ordered that you could be taken to court and punished for simply sitting in the wrong chair at the dinner table in your own house! No wonder people in such feudal societies made a blessing of obedience, an aesthetic of poverty. These limitations make up a good part of our Zen inheritance. Still, the positive aspects remain. There is beauty to be found in the art of making do. Like the haiku poetry in this book, Zen wisdom bursts forth from the limitations imposed upon it.

BEAUTY IN CONSTRAINT

The idea of limits is appalling to Americans. Think about it. Nothing and no one seems to have the right to constrain us. We spend a good part of our lives fighting against limits. We see them as challenges to overcome—poverty, illness, every dysfunction you can think of, and even some you haven't thought of. America is teeming with such champions. Sure, it shows we've got a strong will and a creative spirit, and these are necessary in confronting life-and-death challenges. But that's not what it takes in living with the limitations of our everyday experiences: not getting that vacation when you wanted it; or that course you wanted to teach so badly; or that client who seemed so ready to sign on. Limitations are our life. There is beauty in constraint, not merely in challenging it, but in becoming one with it.

Where is the constraint once you've become one with it? Do you rail against the breath for being limited to an inhalation followed by an exhalation? Do you refuse the moment because it limits you to being sick instead of healthy, or confined to a small apartment instead of a mansion?

Instead of trying to fend off limitations, it's better just to be one hundred percent limited. It's not easy, but we can take comfort in the knowledge that the next moment always contains something new. As we discovered early on in our life together, this is especially important when it comes to building and maintaining a relationship.

BUILDING A SPIRITUAL PARTNERSHIP

Having volunteered to join the crew that was building a new Zen temple for our community in Hawai'i, we found ourselves on a mountainside one day, crouching next to each other with machete in hand, cutting our way through a dense tropical forest. Neither of us had any building experience, and, finding the heat and the mosquitoes almost unbearable, we were tempted to drop our machetes and take off. But being known around the Zen center as the "Dynamic Duo" had given us a reputation to uphold. So, after exchanging an "I'd-rather-die-than-quit" look and taking a drink out of our canteens, we continued slashing away. Then one day we got the idea that the job might be easier if we turned it into a form of meditation. We decided to work without talking unless it was necessary, and to concentrate on our breathing as we focused our attention, moment- by-moment, on our activities. The difference between meditating at the Zen center and building a temple together was that here, on the mountainside, instead of sitting individually on our cushions, we'd be working and "meditating in tandem." Inspired by a simile from our favorite Zen poet, Ikkyu, we started by counting our exhalations and visualizing ourselves "as two limbs of a single tree"—that is, functionally separate but joined at the trunk. Our experiment had an immediate, and positive, impact on our work and our meditation practice. Working meditatively as partners had not only doubled the intensity and power of attention we'd achieved by meditating as individuals, it also revealed that physical limitations were excellent opportunities for Zen practice!

It took six months to clear the path through that jungle; and it was a year before we could actually break ground. Building on a mountainside in a rain forest, directly in the path of mudslides, added further complications even after we did break ground. And it took another six months before we could pour the foundation. It seemed that every step forward was followed by two steps back. No sooner would we frame the first building than the humidity would warp some important beam or other, and we'd have to take down the whole frame and start all over again. It was frustrating. But so was sitting in zazen alone on your cushions in the zendo. You'd no sooner settle into a "groove" and get really concentrated, than your stomach would start growling. You were hungry. You were starving. You fantasized about what the cook was making for dinner. You wanted to steal a look at your watch to see how long it was until dinner. You couldn't move. But being hungry had somehow interfered with your comfortable seat, and now your ankle was hurting. All your best and most concentrated efforts flew out the window. Start again. From counting the breaths. One . . . two . . . three . . .

Working together on that construction site proved no less spiritual, and no less difficult, than sitting in meditation. Moreover, building the temple provided the tools and the hands-on experience we would need to get through the complex emotional tangle of relationship awaiting us in the months that followed. Even more important, it gave us the blueprint for living in the "real world" as everyday married people who were no longer residents at a Zen center. Buying a condo and setting up house together, we learned soon enough that "two limbs of a single tree" often faced in opposite directions and crowded each other's space. For example, we'd take the painstaking step of clearing away a temperamental "weed" in our relationship—say, negotiating a compromise in a heated debate over where to put a piece of furniture—and overnight, a new temperamental "weed" would pop up in its place. We'd be ready to start "breaking ground," hoping to reach new levels of intimacy, only to find ourselves talking past each other. Again, we could just as well have dropped our tools and called it quits. But we didn't, because we both knew that what we were building together wasn't just an ordinary "house" but a "temple," not just an ordinary relationship, but a spiritual partnership. After five years of marriage, we realized that the very act of building that partnership was itself our spiritual practice.

It's been almost ten years since we left Hawai'i and established our own Zen center on the Mainland, but we still consider Honolulu "home" and return there often. We especially like to drive up the long, winding road in the Palolo Valley to have a look at the temple we helped build. The kitchen still isn't finished, but the meditation hall is standing firm. The huge elephant-leaf plants and creeping vines have been freshly cut away, but you can tell that they're still threatening to grow back into jungle. No matter how neatly you try to arrange it, life refuses patterning. It prefers to amble along in a messy sprawl. But that doesn't mean you stop building. You learn how to work *with* it, rather than *on* it, adjusting your blueprint as you go.

It's the same with building a relationship. You may have to frame it several times before it's strong enough to wear its outer skin of bricks and mortar. Sometimes a storm will come and knock the whole thing down, and you'll have to start from scratch. The important thing is that you stick with whatever you're doing in the moment. That way, whatever is going on between you and your partner becomes the context of your relationship manifesting as the storm. There's no need to analyze it; instead you simply weather it by letting go of your thoughts and attending to the space you're in right there and then. Don't label it "good" or "bad," a "turn-on" or a "turn-off." Don't try to repress it, and don't hold onto it. Be aware that the limitation you are experiencing is a passing condition and it will change, for change is the only certainty you can rely on.

In my native place

there's this plant:

as plain as grass

but blooms like heaven

—Issas

SACRED SPACE

Rituals

Considering that Grassroots Zen is secular and practiced outside of the monastery, it would seem that there's no need for creating rituals or making "sacred space." If Zen is none other than eating, sleeping, working, and caring for our families, then aren't we practicing all the time? Yes, but it's precisely because Zen makes no distinctions between traditional notions of "holy" and "unholy" that we sometimes get diverted from experiencing the holiness of the ordinary. We get lazy, like the lawyer we knew in Hawai'i, a longtime practitioner who, when asked why he no longer attended sesshin, replied, "I'm practicing all the time, whether I'm arguing a case in court or sitting on my lanai drinking beer, it's all Zen." Not surprisingly, we heard from friends that within a year the lawyer had stopped sitting altogether. That's why ritual is important; it creates a Zen environment, sets the scene for focusing attention. And focusing attention is the first step in becoming one with the moment.

We've thought a long time about the kinds of rituals that might be appropriate to grassroots practitioners who don't necessarily think of themselves as Buddhists. Our Princeton grassroots sangha is comfortable with some of the rituals we inherited from traditional Japanese Zen, and in integrating them we've created our own Zen environment without, as one of our members put it, "throwing out the baby with the bath water." Every Western grassroots center is different in the way it handles the rituals that came to us from the East. Some adhere to them entirely, others blend Christian, Jewish, and Buddhist ceremonies, and still others, while divesting themselves of every trace of Buddhist ritual, have developed new forms appropriate to their particular way of practicing. But no matter how it's done, it's impossible to practice without some sort of ritual.

LOVING ATTENTION

We Grassroots Zen practitioners are in the enviable position of creating our own rituals. As we mature in Zen, we mature in its expression. We develop greater self-confidence and, in most cases, an even stronger passion for the practice than we had when we first began to sit. We approach the cushions as we would approach a meeting with a lover. Delighting in each gesture, we prepare the setting: place flowers in a vase and set it on the altar, fluff the cushions, light the incense. We look forward with excitement to that daily meeting. It's special because it takes place early in the morning or late in the evening and is limited to twenty-five minutes or, if we're lucky, an hour. We steal time with our "beloved" in the course of a busy day. Gradually we learn to carry that loving attention into our daily routine. Everything is set aglow when you're in love; we all know the feeling. Even the most mundane activities are invested with the radiance of our early morning encounter on the cushions.

Wherever we are, whatever we're doing, we carry our ardor with us.

SETTING THE SCENE

Dress is an important aspect of ritual. Some people like to wear dark colors when they sit. Others like to wear a particular article of clothing as a special reminder. Sitting at home together every Sunday, for example, we put on our *rakusus*—a *rakusu* is the short black bib representing the monk's surplice—that were presented to us by our teacher when we took the Buddhist precepts. But those are the only times we wear our *rakusus*. Out of habit, we might wear dark colors when we're sitting formally with our group, but we don't wear traditional Zen attire in the zendo.

Grassroots practitioners generally choose their own rituals for sitting at home. An artist friend has placed a stone and a piece of driftwood on a small table in front of her cushion in a corner of her living room. A loving father keeps his ten-year-old daughter's drawing of him on his altar. To commemorate special occasions, a husband and wife read a poem aloud together. Once, when we were guests at a home zendo in the country, we were treated to a round of walking meditation in the garden. When we have houseguests who sit, we invite them to join us. Arranging the space in our basement zendo to please our friends, we take out our "guest cushions," light a candle and incense, and chant the Heart Sutra.

A LANGUAGE OF BEING

Anyone can make "plain grass bloom like heaven." When a friend who travels a lot on business complained of the "un-Zenlike atmosphere" of his hotel rooms, we told him what we do when we're on the road. Since we like traveling light, we don't bring along our cushions. We turn our hotel room into a "sacred space" by using blankets and pillows instead of mats and cushions and by clapping our hands instead of using a bell to keep time.

Ritual has its own logic. It's about being rather than doing. Its language is nonlinear, designed to appeal to the senses rather than to the intellect. That's why so many of the Sino-Japanese chants, even when translated into English, have no syntactical meaning. The experience of moving the vocal chords in time with the breath is more important than understanding what we're chanting. Chanting without attention to "meaning" puts us into the nonlinear, nondualistic frame of mind that seeds awakening. It's said that the illiterate Chinese rice polisher who became the great sixth ancestor of Zen was enlightened on hearing the Diamond Sutra chanted in the marketplace without intellectually "understanding" a word of it.

Ritual allows for the fusion of subject and object. It is experiential, transformative, timeless. Symbols of personal and group meaning help us focus unselfconsciously on what we feel good about. But we need a healthy sense of self to start with, so it helps to create our own rituals. We perform them because they give us pleasure while at the same time relaxing the ego's hold on us. Losing the self in a ritual is a prelude to experiencing the sacred in the ordinary. Ritual is the art of cultivating attention. It ought to be something we do lovingly, with care.

Shared symbols make for meaningful group rituals; private symbols offer a personal link to their enactment. Bodhidharma, the eighth-century founder of Zen in China, exemplifies this in his role as creator of the green-tea ritual that has been associated with Zen ever since. According to the legend, Bodhidharma grew the first little green-tea bush outside his cave and gave his students the leaves to chew on so they wouldn't fall asleep while doing zazen. Eventually, this became formalized as a ritual. Whether it's the tea ceremony in Japan or drinking tea in the morning during sesshin, ever since Bodhidharma's time, Zen practitioners have been participating in a communal ritual that simultaneously serves a very practical function. Whether we do it formally, sitting in the zendo and pouring tea into Japanese cups, or whether we gather around the urn at the buffet table in silence, each filling our own mug with tea and sitting down to drink it in the living room or on the porch, we are performing a Zen ritual that physically and emotionally strengthens our resolve to practice Bodhidharma's way together.

SYMBOLIC GESTURES

Ritual must have a physical component, even if it's only a small symbolic gesture, like lighting incense before taking to the cushion. Or it can be feeding the cat or making the bed mindfully, quieting our thoughts, waking up out of the world of mindless actions into focused, concentrated awareness. All these small awareness rituals can be what the Buddha called "skillful means" for opening to the moment. The energy built up in our own private sitting rituals accumulates and empowers us as a group when we share together, in common, ancient Zen rituals like drinking tea. They enhance our zazen and expand our capacity for awareness. It's the same with chanting. Even those of us who've chanted the same verses for years are enjoined to chant them as if for the first time. This goes for small, everyday gestures too. The more mindful we are of the way we open and close a door, the less likely we'll be to let it slam shut behind us. Not only because we're aware that someone may be resting or meditating in the zendo during a break, but also because we've accustomed ourselves to making sacred spaces in our minds even when we're at home.

When "inside and outside become one," zazen is no longer just another chore. Nor is it a great spiritual achievement. We sit simply to relish the experience of sitting. We perform a ritual because we are *moved* to perform it, not because we have to or are expected to. There's no one there to mete out punishment if we do it "wrong." We won't get brownie points for doing it "right." We aren't looking over our shoulder to see if anyone's noticed how gracefully we bow or how saintly we look as we're lighting the incense. In the end, it's we ourselves who must make our "native place" bloom like heaven.

THE MIDDLE WAY

AVOIDING EXTREMES

The Buddha struck upon the Middle Way after having gone through two extreme phases in his life. During the first phase, he was raised as a prince and lived in a palace where he was sheltered from sickness, old age, and death. In the second phase, he lived in the jungle and practiced a variety of harsh ascetic disciplines until he almost died. Finally giving up these practices, he sat under the Bodhi tree in meditation and attained realization. Afterward, he embarked upon his own version of the "Middle Way." For the Buddha, this consisted of gathering a sangha, a wandering community of fellow meditators; teaching about the beginning and end of suffering, which he referred to as the Four Noble Truths; and living as a monk without indulging in extreme austerities.

By today's standards, the Buddha's Middle Way still looks pretty ascetic. Nonetheless, in avoiding extremes, it provides a model to those of us who practice Grassroots Zen. Taking our cue from Buddha Shakyamuni, we, too, have to find our Middle

Way. To be authentic in our practice, we don't have to slavishly imitate the life of the Buddha or, for that matter, that of an ancient Chinese or Japanese Zen master. But the message is the same for us as it was for them: find a Middle Way you can live with. Avoid the extremes of perfection. Don't become a "perfect sitter" at the expense of other dimensions in your life. In fact, don't try to become perfect at anything you do. If you manage to avoid becoming perfect, you'll be embarking on the Middle Way.

There's so much more to life than just one role. We have many roles, and we're called upon, first, to balance them and, second, to experience new ones; we never fully "get there," never achieve perfection in the sense of arriving somewhere and resting there. We rest in the unfolding of being; it's a dynamic rest, never the rest of static achievement. It's always moving back and forth between extremes, so it can only be experienced as the Middle Way. We're never just rich or just poor or just old or just young. We're a mixture of all these things. It may be different for each of us, but it's still a mixture, and we have to find our balance in it.

We must always ask ourselves where this balance lies. This is something we have to work on every day; and it's new each time. It's not as if we find a Middle Way for all occasions and that's the end of it. Our Middle Way is always shifting. There are always different circumstances coming our way, demanding revisions of our original plans. As life takes unexpected turns, we have to ask ourselves, "What do I do now?" "Where's the Middle Way at this moment?"

FINDING BALANCE

To be extreme is to be unbalanced and to lose the Middle Way, as the Buddha himself learned. He didn't find peace of mind in his father's palace, nor did he find it in the jungle. He found peace of mind only when he found his own balance.

Finding your balance is like finding the rhythm of your life. Once you've found it, you're no longer as judgmental or demanding. You stop driving yourself. As you ease up on yourself, you understand that although you're never going to be perfect, you'll also never be an absolute failure. It's more likely that you'll be something in-between.

A single twenty-five-minute meditation period perfectly illustrates how zazen can lead to the Middle Way. We focus on the breath, then we stray from it; we return to the breath, then stray again. Back and forth, back and forth, neither scolding ourselves for not staying with the breath nor escaping into daydreams. The Middle Way of zazen consists of gently coming back to the breath over and over again. It teaches us tolerance for ourselves and others. It leads us to openness and understanding. "Ice and water forgetting their old difference"—that's our Middle Way.

ALWAYS PRACTICING

We like the Mahayana claim that the Buddha himself is always practicing. Dogen phrased it beautifully when he said, "The green mountains are always walking." Note that in both cases the emphasis is on *always*. There's never a time when the Buddha, the universe, is not practicing. The beauty of the practice of the Middle Way is that it is never-ending. There are very few religious philosophies that appreciate or fully accept this "not quite getting there." The Middle Way reveals that in the very condition of "not quite getting there," we're already there. We're no longer judging and asking ourselves these questions: "Why am I not perfect?" "Why don't I have a great enlightenment experience like the ones I've read about?" "Why do I have only one little insight when I could have ten?" "Why do I always get angry?" "Why am I not more 'Zen-like'?" "Why am I not more soft-spoken?" "Why do I still like beer?" Sound familiar? Despite all this, the Middle Way makes it possible for us to accept ourselves as we are. We just keep practicing and suddenly, without whipping ourselves, change happens!

There's no need to drive ourselves, because change happens on its own. It comes with an embrace of the Middle Way that each of us has to discover every day over and over again. It's never the same. How do you know when you've found it? That's another one of those dangerous questions. If you need to know your Middle Way, as the punchline of a popular koan puts it, "the arrow has already flown past Korea." The Middle Way isn't so much a matter of knowing or not knowing as it is about walking on—*always* walking on. A good way to try it is in walking meditation. As your first foot touches the ground, are you there? Are you open? Are you at rest while moving? Are you criticizing the way you walk? Do you have a running commentary going on about the scenery? Or can you drop it and start again, one foot in front of the other? The Middle Way is there in that next step.

ZEN EXPERIENCE

Zen experience consists of truly meeting the moment, not just in our heads but with every fiber of our being. It's really quite ordinary. We find it in the smile that comes to the old student Mahakashyapa's face when he sees the Buddha twirling a flower during a dharma talk. For no reason at all, the Zen student simply smiles as she walks out in the morning and sees the neighbor's orange cat sitting on the front porch railing licking its paws. A flower, a cat—everything perfect as it is—there's the Middle Way. So is straying off course, losing your balance and returning again to the moment.

Zen experience offers a different kind of perfection from the one we've been brought up to believe in. It isn't linear: it doesn't evolve to an endpoint and we don't progress toward it. That way of looking at perfection demands a lot of checking. We're nervous, always looking over our shoulder to see how far we've gotten. "There" is inevitably far away from "here." It's got to be different from everything that went on before. Our Western, Judeo–Christian upbringing doesn't make it easy for us to accept that the perfection of the Middle Way has no beginning and no end, that it's right here, unfolding with the moment.

Sad and joyous moments, successful and unsuccessful moments, every conceivable moment—the Middle Way encompasses them all. There is no "Point Omega" to reach. We live our lives fully, and that's it. Those of us who like philosophizing can read any number of purposes into life; there's nothing wrong with that. Life is a very interesting story. But we shouldn't read too much into it, nor should we turn it into a rigid set of rules and regulations. As long as we just play, live out our stories with the unself-consciousness of a child embarking on a new adventure, we'll be okay. There's no need to worry; we can always count on our breath to bring us safely to the Middle Way.

THE FOUR ABODES

COMPASSION AND EQUANIMITY

According to the Buddha, the awakened person dwells in the "Four Abodes" of equanimity, loving-kindness, sympathetic joy, and compassion. These four desired psychological conditions resulting from meditation practice all reflect each other. Equanimity is part of compassion; there is no sympathetic joy without loving-kindness, and so on. There's really no special order of importance to the Four Abodes, so, rather than tease them apart, we'd like to explore how they're interwoven.

Equanimity has come up in several different contexts in this book. Here we define it as the mirror image of compassion. Interestingly, of the Four Abodes, both equanimity and compassion are the most frequently misunderstood. For those of us growing up in a Judeo-Christian culture, equanimity is usually identified with stoicism, the philosophy of the stiff upper lip. We think of compassion as a form of love. We know what "love" is, but "compassion" somehow just doesn't cut it. It doesn't evoke the powerful images that love does. It's only when we

break off the second syllable that we begin to understand a little better: "Passion." That's something we know well.

Passion is important in Grassroots Zen practice. We emphasize this because most people tend to think of Zen as a practice of complete detachment. At a wedding recently, a Tibetan
Buddhist practitioner we were chatting with told us he liked
Zen but found it rather "stark and austere." Zen people are supposed to be calm, cool, and collected at all times. We don't need
passion because the practice has left us so full and complete
unto ourselves that the world no longer holds any interest for
us, right? Wrong. We reject the idea that maturing in Zen
means ridding ourselves of emotions, of passion. And we have
no intention of shedding these as we would a set of old clothes.
We also don't practice in order to emerge into some final stage
of perfect, pure, and pristine detachment. Then how do we
dwell in the Four Abodes?

The passion that's most obvious in our grassroots sangha is
the affection we feel for each other. We feel gratitude for being
together, nourishing and sustaining each other in our grassy
field of practice, our world. We acknowledge this each time we
bow or walk in meditation together, drink tea, or offer each
other a cookie and accept or say, "Not tonight, thanks. Doctor
says I have to watch out for my cholesterol." How can we be
separated from feeling that we want tea without a cookie
tonight? How can that be "bad?" It only becomes bad when
we're seen as "immature" or "weird" for refusing the offer of a
cookie. That's when the flow of passion becomes disconnected,
when feelings petrify and we leave off interacting in order to
maintain our safe, rigid sense of self. We want to believe that
we're more "normal," more "mature" than our friend. It's when
we give credence to the substantiality of this "normal,"
"mature" self that we lose sight of the big picture.

THE BIG PICTURE

Compassion means feeling with, desiring with, suffering with, wishing with, sensing with. In other words, the self—the sensing, feeling, suffering, loving self—put into a broader context. Or perhaps we should say, compassion consists of awakening to the fact that we have never left our original abode. It is getting a good look at the big picture, the wide panorama that's been obscured by our refusal to see the self bonded in love to all that exists. As we've repeatedly emphasized, Grassroots Zen practice isn't about detachment. We don't travel inward in order to lose all sense of the outer world. On the contrary, it's about opening up, recognizing connections, experiencing the feelings of others as our own, marveling at what Zen teacher Thich Nhat Hanh calls the vast jeweled net of "interbeing." Transformed by compassion, the self opens up, reconnects to a vibrant, ever-changing universe. Rigid boundaries disappear and walls crumble, giving way to equanimity.

When the self is transformed, feeling with an old man doesn't necessarily mean that a young woman will have to annihilate herself and magically turn into an old man. There's nothing magical about it. She's simply awakening to the big picture she shares with the old man. There's still a sense of self. There's still the almost instinctive recognition of difference, but this difference isn't absolute. The old man and the young woman are connected; there can't be one without the other. There's no you without the person sitting next to you, the seat beneath you, the humming air conditioner, the airplane going by overhead. This sense of contextuality, of broadening the view through the senses, is the way we define compassionate equanimity.

Our identity appears only as part of a context. The very subtle, profound threads connecting us to that context are our senses. Through them we experience the "passions" reminding us that all sentient and insentient beings depend on each other for their existence. It turns out that we humans are, quite literally, "grass roots," one with plants, animals, and even fungi. Scientists have revealed that our family tree is taller and deeper than ever expected. According to Brent Mishler, a botanist at the University of California at Berkeley, "[T]he classic split between the plant and animal kingdoms is incorrect . . . Most of the data show that fungi are actually closer to animals than to other groups . . . In addition, animals, plants and fungi occupy adjacent twigs on the tree of life that overwhelmingly consists of bacteria and other single-celled creatures . . . It's kind of a humbling thing . . . ." Humans and animals and plants and fungi—the more we feel, the more we interact, the more we extend the boundaries of the self, the more at home we are in the universe. We still maintain our own peculiar ways and our own weaknesses. There is never a time when we don't freeze a picture or a moment when we don't wish to be somewhere else; there's never a moment when we don't try to somehow reaffirm that rigid sense of self, but with practice, these moments become more tolerable, and they don't last as long. We cling less when we simply observe, recognize, and feel the urge to freeze the moment, and let it pass through. It's a tough koan for everyone.

We've been working on it especially hard since we've been living out in the cornfields of Central Illinois. We were both raised in cities, so we often find ourselves fantasizing about what it would be like to get back to the city. Mostly we wish we were back home in Honolulu. Will we ever stop wishing we were somewhere else? Probably not. Does having preferences mean we fall short of being *real* Zen practitioners? Actually, preferences aren't the problem. The problem is thinking you know what a *real* Zen practitioner is and measuring yourself against that, rather than really working with what's at hand. And what's at hand in our case is that we wish, that we desire, not just to live in the city, but that we desire, period. The important question to ask is "How are we going to deal with our desire?"

Recently we were driving along on the freeway listening to a tape by the American yogi Ram Dass on this very subject. We looked at each other and smiled when we heard him say, "I constantly find myself wishing that things would be different, or that I'd be someone else, or that I'd be in a different situation. However, the point is not that I ever reach a place where I no longer wish, or feel, or desire, but that I simply begin to recognize that that's what's going on right now. 'Aha! Wishing. Aha! Desiring. That's okay.'"

Of course we have to draw a line; we can't simply let ourselves be dragged along by our desires, act out, maybe hurt others. Granted, it's a fine line. But more often than not, we're too hard on ourselves. We think we know where and who we should be, because we think we know what *real* Zen practice entails. The truth is, we don't know. We can't, because, as so many koans remind us, the dharma isn't a matter of knowing or not knowing. The dharma is the big picture in which we find ourselves. It includes sensing, thinking, feeling, interacting; it can't be boiled down to a single formula. We can't be boiled down to a single formula either. There's no such thing as a real Zen practitioner. Yet there is effort, practice. We are moving toward something. What? A process of more awareness, greater understanding of the nature of self, a recognition of interdependence. And this understanding translates into "compassion": feeling with, being with, suffering with, living with, loving with. Zen is about that process. It does not have an absolute goal, because there is no goal. Every time we think we've caught it, it's moved, changed right under our very noses.

But there is awareness. The less aware we are, the more difficult life becomes. The more rules we create, the more intolerant we become. Nonetheless, embodying Ram Dass's warning and simply observing, "Aha! Intolerance" will transform that intolerance into compassion. It will broaden our sense of identity. It will eliminate the bad taste of not having lived up to what we were supposed to be, of not being worth much. Awareness lets us chuckle at ourselves: "Okay, there I go again."

Compassion is the self facing the challenges posed by the practice, listening to another person's problems, finding twenty-five minutes to sit every day, making a phone call, offering a ride to the zendo to someone without a car. That's when we leave our little, circumscribed self behind and open up to the rich grassy field of our context wherever it is. Compassion is truly our central concern. There's no equanimity without compassion and, because they can't be separated, no compassion without equanimity. They're one and the same. To be equanimous is to be compassionate—to feel with, suffer with. It's a process, ongoing, unending. That's what makes it so rewarding.

LOVING-KINDNESS AND SYMPATHETIC JOY

Loving-kindness and sympathetic joy, which are the culmination of compassion and equanimity, aren't usually associated with Zen because they seem to imply devotion, and Zen is not a "devotional practice." It doesn't encourage worship of a beloved teacher, image, or person or the complete loss of dualistic consciousness that occurs in such a relationship. Still, loving-kindness and sympathetic joy have a central place in our Grassroots Zen practice—not as submission or emotional devotion, but as "care." In our discussion of time, we talked about caring for the moment as you would care for a newborn. Applied from the vantage point of space, loving-kindness is caring for the moment manifesting as the impermanent self. Caring for ourselves as the moment and realizing our interdependence naturally results in sympathetic joy. When we experience others as no other than ourselves, how can we not take delight in our neighbor's joy? It's not really so esoteric. You don't have to be a saint. All you have to do to see a reflexive expression of loving-kindness and sympathetic joy is to sit across from a couple with a smiling infant in a basket at the airport and look at the faces of the passengers sitting next to them. Everyone, if even for a few seconds, stops what they're doing and delights in that baby. This is what it is to be fully human.

This joyful experience begins with an understanding of who we are, of how this bodymind works, of how we react and feel in the moment. It happens when, instead of separating ourselves, we give our full attention to the smiling baby. Note that we said "attention" not "observation." It's only during those moments when we refrain from the knee-jerk impulse to dissociate ourselves from the world, when we're caught off guard, so to speak, that we can really care. And this caring is the spontaneous expression of the self as loving-kindness and sympathetic joy. The mind becomes one with the act of "caring," reflecting everything that appears. So if Buddha appears in the form of a smiling baby, Buddha is reflected. By letting this reflection truly sink in, by actually *becoming* that reflection, we truly meet the moment, gain an understanding of the self in its context and in its relationship with other beings. There's a double bonus at such moments: in expressing loving-kindness toward the baby, we can begin to feel it for ourselves. We can, however briefly, ease up on ourselves, stop being so harsh to the moment. Unfortunately life in our competitive society doesn't let this come easily.

It's alarming to see how mean-spirited we've become. Instead of feeling sympathetic joy, we seem to be taking more and more pleasure in the harm suffered by others. Whether it be a football player punched in the groin in full view of millions of onlookers, or a tiny dog tossed down the garbage chute of a high-rise building, or a wrestler falling to his death in a badly executed flying stunt, American film and television audiences can't seem to get enough. During a discussion of television violence, a student in one of our classes at the university shamefacedly admitted that he studied while watching people "go at each other" on *The Jerry Springer Show*. His admission was followed by an enthusiastic chorus, each student detailing his or her favorite form of "trashing." Looking back on our violent twentieth century, it's particularly worrisome to see young people taking such glee in cruelty. If the gladiatorial society is a promise of things to come in the twenty-first century, we'll have to practice caring that much more.

EASING UP

It doesn't really matter whether or not we reach all our goals and objectives, even the spiritual ones. What is important, though, is the way we treat the moment. When we treat it as an object, we are being tough on ourselves, which inevitably brings much pain and suffering into our lives. We can't rest; we feel alienated, frustrated, disappointed. And instead of letting the disappointment reflect itself, we punish ourselves in the struggle to run away from it. We hate ourselves for being disappointed. Then for being angry. Then for being depressed. It never ends. That road leads directly to more and more and more suffering. It also leads to less loving-kindess, less sympathetic joy, and ultimately to less compassion, not only for ourselves but for everyone and everything around us.

Because of its connection to the Japanese samurai tradition, Zen has earned a reputation for harshness. In returning to the older Chinese "grassroots" style of practice, we've chosen to emphasize its nonmilitary, nonmonastic side. The ordinary lay practitioner is better served in bringing Zen into our own backyards, practicing, literally and figuratively, at home. We grow together in the grassy field of our society, cultivating loving-kindness by caring, paying attention to those with whom we share the world. If we truly become aware of our actions, we don't need to be forced to grow. It happens very naturally. If we truly become aware of our anger, of our disappointment, there's a sudden opening, an acceptance that offers the chance to stop carrying those feelings around with us. There's no longer the need to hold on, struggle, push away, dissociate ourselves from rising thoughts, feelings, conditions, or moments. They simply come and go, as naturally as the changing seasons.

As soon as we care for the moment, we allow loving-kindness and sympathetic joy to enter. We care for our relationships, we're willing to experience what's going on right now, including the psychological stuff that comes up. Sometimes this stuff will be overwhelming, but even then, we can practice by not blowing it out of proportion. We're not denying that it's the psychological stuff that's most often the hardest to practice with. People always ask us how they can practice loving-kindness and sympathetic joy with those they dislike intensely. The only response we can give comes from our personal experience of trying our best not to pump it up. It's so easy to give that balloon an endless supply of hot air. We're both fiery types, so living together has given us plenty of practice in this department. We've even made an agreement that when we fight, there are certain lines we won't cross, hurtful things we won't say. And it works.

Of course, this is only possible in a loving relationship. But what about when you're faced by someone who really wishes you ill or even actively persecutes you? The only thing you can do in that case is work on not letting the situation get out of hand. Talk about it with someone you trust; listen to the advice of other people; don't put yourself in a situation where it's likely that the relationship will grow worse; don't offer any possible points of contention. Seek to neutralize the relationship. In such situations, loving-kindness means you're willing to work with whatever comes up, not just to give in and follow your own worst impulse to destruction or annihilation of the other person by alienating yourself from her or by just ignoring what's going on. That won't work. Closing off is not our practice.

Zen is about opening up. It's about fully inhabiting the sacred space of the moment. Breathing, listening to the sounds, feeling the air on your skin: all this is opening to the realm of perception, the true self, and realizing the fundamental interdependence of all things. Since nothing is disconnected from anything else, loving-kindness is recognizing that fundamental interdependence, even when it is manifesting as conflict. Interdependence is just another name for compassion, loving-kindness, sympathetic joy, and equanimity. They're all branches of the single grass root we call the Buddha Way.

motion

EMOTION

BEING HUMAN

What we call the "self" is actually a changing spatial pattern made by the movement of time. Leaving no tracks, it nonetheless manifests temporarily as the qualities of bending, resisting, connecting, and unfolding. The self in motion is life for life's sake, "a butterfly wandering down the city street."

The absence of physical motion is the most obvious aspect of sitting meditation. For the busy grassroots practitioner, "just sitting" can be very demanding. But coping with the motion of the mind is still harder. Once we've managed this, it's easier to deal with our emotions, to know when to yield, when to persist, when to slow down, and when to speed up.

There's no getting around it. Even with all the changes we've made, Zen is still perceived by many newcomers as an austere, cold, nondevotional practice. They wonder how such "juicy," engaged, passionate people can find emotional satisfaction in sitting and facing the wall. We hear this a lot from people who've come from other, more devotional meditative

Buddhist traditions. They see Zen as an "unemotional" practice without a heart. To a certain degree, there's truth to this. Zen is not a practice that consciously utilizes emotions to bring about some particular state of mind. At the same time, it takes emotions very seriously. In fact, Zen without emotions is impossible, since it's about us as complete human beings and there's no such thing as an emotionless human being. If Zen is about living our lives moment by moment, how can emotions be excluded? We find this out from our very first experience of zazen.

BODYMIND EVENTS

The first piece of advice we give when we teach people how to sit is, "Let your emotions, your feelings, come and go. Don't hold onto them and don't reject them." Like all the other sensations we experience as we sit—smelling the incense, feeling the temperature in the room on our skin, seeing the light on the wall through partly closed eyes—emotions are the fabric of our practice. They are no different from all the other bodymind events going on during each twenty-five-minute period on our cushions. Instead of focusing on them, we're better served if we let our emotions blend in naturally with the other sensations. It's easier to do if we regard thinking as our sixth sense.

As the mind begins to settle, as we start to let go of our dualistic, conceptual thinking and focus our attention on the breath, we no longer have to regard our emotions as something apart from us. We're no longer driven by them because we don't have the time or the leisure to indulge them. The process in zazen usually starts out with the sensation of a particular emotion. Recall our earlier description of the emergence of hatred. Since anger is so closely related to hatred, and because it comes up more often than sheer hatred, let's look at the sensory origins of anger. Under ordinary circumstances, by the time we realize that we feel anger, it has grown to such an extent that it's almost impossible to let go of. We're completely suffused by it. The anger is so heavy, so much part of us, that there simply is no dropping it.

Zazen allows us the time and the space to pay attention to the anger as it journeys into motion. We see how it picks up steam, expands, and tries to take hold of us. Again, the point here is not to divorce ourselves from the anger as if it were some alien bodysnatcher come from outer space to invade us. We experience the emotion as part of our context, of what's going on right now. No different from hearing a sound, it charges a sensation, a bodymind event. Like that sound, because the emotion is very much part of us, we don't shut it out. When we break down the walls that divide us from our sensory world, the context and its emotional component become sharper. But because we concentrate on a single point, such as the breath, it's much easier for us to let the bodymind do its thing without the ego getting in the way and manipulating the process.

It's a little bit like swimming in the ocean. When you swim out a bit, you flip over on your back and let the waves carry you. Thanks to the salt water, you can float without having to move around and do very much. You sense the same life throbbing through the water that's throbbing through your body. You become part of the currents, experiencing their changing motions as your own. If you close your eyes it becomes impossible to tell where the water ends and you begin. You and your context are one and the same. Yet there's a stillness in all this movement, complete relaxation. And though there's very little thought, you're still fully there, fully present, fully alive.

What happens during zazen when those waves of "emotion" begin to roll? We're completely relaxed, floating with the breath. The emotions come; sometimes they're strong, sometimes they're weak. We don't suppress them, we don't fight them. It's this that people very often don't understand about zazen: our practice doesn't entail repressing emotions. We're not sitting in order to deaden our bodies or numb our minds into insensibility. Quite the contrary. When we're fully absorbed in zazen, the whole body *becomes* emotion. We're still there with the breath, sometimes diverted from it, of course, but always returning to it. The ocean of emotions is always flowing, always carrying us. Good floaters can continue to remain on their backs even when the big waves come.

Strictly speaking, we're not studying emotions so much as paying attention to them. There's nothing discursive or analytical about our practice. We simply pay attention to the never-ending motions of the bodymind. There's much to learn from letting emotions come and go. But because it's such an intimate experience, it can't be taught. We each have to experience it for ourselves.

Often when we find ourselves getting angry or sad or upset over something, there's that little sense of recognition, what we like to call "Ram Dass's 'Aha!'" We know that particular emotion well from our sitting. We've experienced it, let it come and go, gotten pretty good at not letting it drag us around as much as it used to. This isn't a rejection of our emotion but a refusal to exaggerate its importance.

Too many Westerners are in the habit of psychologizing everything. One of our Japanese Zen teachers used to joke about this by announcing, "I'm putting out my shingle" before giving dokusan (student interviews). Since we're not trained as professional therapists, we have no problem telling students right away that we're not qualified to analyze their emotions. All we can do is show them how to work with them as they come up in zazen. The Buddha often talked about the many components that make up our experience. He's very clear about the fact that emotions, though important, are only part of that experience. Taking the Buddha's advice, we can't go wrong if we see emotions as only one part of the entire context of our practice, no more and no less. In order to do this, we have to maintain a feeling for the overall structure, the interdependence of things.

It might be easier to realize how a thought comes and goes, but it's typically very hard to realize the transitoriness of emotions because they appear to be so monolithic, so powerful. It's hard to resist them. Yet they're the same as thoughts. They're just as evanescent. It's good to keep reminding ourselves that—like smell, taste, touch, seeing, and hearing—emotions are also part of our sensory apparatus. In fact, their very existence depends on those senses. They all rise and fall together.

A TOTAL EXPERIENCE

Because we see Zen practice as a total experience, we don't put special emphasis on emotions. There isn't anything more important about them than there is about the sound of the garbage truck outside. Both are wonderful manifestations of the Buddha Way, gateways to learning about the true nature of the self. Both reflect who and what we are at a particular moment. In a given context, the sound of a pebble hitting the pavement might be more "important" than the exquisite welling up of an emotion. When we sit, we sit as full and complete beings. When we have an emotionally challenging period, that's our context, and we take it seriously. When we're having sleepy zazen, then that's our context, our challenge, and we take it seriously too.

There are many forms of meditation, and it's foolish to try to prove any one better than any other. All have their strengths and weaknesses. The important thing for Grassroots Zen practitioners is that we don't try to turn zazen into something that it's not, merely to accommodate the fad of the month. People have to find the practice that best suits their needs and temperaments.

One woman who appeared very early on in the forming of our Princeton group was a really gifted Zen student. She could sit comfortably cross-legged on her cushion for long periods of zazen and showed an affinity for koan practice. Yet, after only one year, it became clear that she missed her church and had only come to Zen because she couldn't find a Christian meditation teacher. We referred her to a group led by a priest who teaches Christian contemplation, and she's very happy there. Instead of trying to rope people into practicing Zen, we'd rather help match them up with the practice that suits them best.

The heart of Zen is the practice of sitting meditation, zazen. It's not devotional, nor does it emphasize emotions over any other aspect of our human experience. Zazen is a vehicle for attaining self-realization in and as the moment. To ask that it deal exclusively with emotions is unrealistic. It would distort the practice. Zazen includes emotions because we breathe with the unfolding moment and discover our connection to the many beings. That's the unadorned Grassroots Zen experience in a nutshell.

PERHAPS THIS VOICELESS

WANDERER DREAMS

OF FLOWERS . . .

BUTTERFLY DOZER

REIKAN

SPIRITUAL HUNGER

LONGING FOR HOME

We once returned from our winter vacation in Hawai'i, where it was eighty-three degrees and sunny, to a blizzard and a temperature of three degrees above zero in Illinois. It was stunning to see how, in only ten hours, our condition had changed so drastically. The snow delayed our commuter flight out of Chicago by four hours, so we had plenty of time to talk about it. Touring the airport to keep awake, we went from one food concession to the next, having tea in one, an apple in another, a soft pretzel in a third, and so on. After doing three rounds of the terminal, we'd had enough. Everywhere we looked, there was food. Too much food. A lot of it was tossed into the trash cans or thoughtlessly left uneaten on the tables. Reminded of the homeless men we'd seen on the beaches in Honolulu eating picnic leftovers right out of the garbage pails, our conversation moved to the subject of hunger.

Most Grassroots Zen practitioners are far removed from hunger. Very few of us have experienced this drastic condition over a sustained period of time. We've seen it on the streets in our cities and towns, read about it in books and newspapers, and some of us might have heard about it from our parents or grandparents who lived through the Great Depression. Others have traveled through less developed countries and witnessed it on a large scale, still only experiencing secondhand what it means to be hungry.

Physical hunger is a state in which the body longs for suste-nance, sometimes so intensely that the longing turns into pain. The body needs to be sustained and nourished in order to func-tion, to grow, to remain in balance. Life and nourishment are inextricably linked. Spiritual hunger is a longing to finally come home; it's a condition in which the bodymind longs for peace. We all know the phrase "peace of mind." Spiritual hunger is the longing for that peace of mind. It's a longing that is sometimes experienced so intensely, that, like physical hunger, it actually hurts. Spiritual hunger also requires nourishment and sustenance.

While food satisfies physical hunger, spiritual hunger is only sated by immersion in the moment, with all its perceptions, mental reactions, thoughts, feelings, emotions, colors, sounds, smells, tastes, and so on. Spiritual food is the wondrous patch-work that we call the moment, the world. This is the context of spiritual hunger. Ironically, it's those who have plenty to eat who are most often spiritually starved. The Dalai Lama notes this when he speaks of traveling through wealthy industrial-ized countries where people are surrounded by luxury and comforts yet beset by forms of anxiety and depression that aren't found in less-developed societies.

In Hakuin's *Song of Zazen,* the image of a person stand-ing in the middle of the water crying out in thirst poignantly describes this condition. Surrounded by the nourishment of the world, we still remain hungry. We are "voiceless wander-ers dreaming of flowers." We think that spiritual hunger has nothing to do with the physical hunger of a homeless man eating out of a garbage pail. We imagine spiritual food to be something special, removed from the ordinariness of our lives, miraculous manna from heaven, some extraordinary manifestation that transcends the world of space, time, and motion. We think it will shatter everything we've known before. It will allow us insight into an entirely different world from the one we live in. We believe that only such an experience will satisfy our spiritual hunger.

Actually, the reason we remain hungry is that we refuse to eat. Perhaps it's better to say that it's not refusal but ignorance. We don't know that our spiritual food is right here, in the everyday moments of our everyday lives. Why don't we know that? The best response is to take a deep breath, then another, then another. This is how the question resolves itself. We don't know that our spiritual food is right here because we don't live in our everyday moments, and because we take conceptual reality, which is only one side of the picture, for the whole picture. We forget, we don't realize that every concept, idea, and thought dissolves in the breath. This is where spiritual hunger and the practice of zazen come together.

APPETITE, HUNGER, AND THIRST

It's very important to be spiritually hungry, really hungry, not just to have an appetite or an inclination, the way you might have a yen for chocolate. Spiritual hunger isn't a matter of "Let's try a little bit of this, a little bit of that, and see how they taste." It won't be satisfied by trying out that new flavor of Ben 'n' Jerry's frozen yogurt or that outrageously priced truffle your friend sent you from France.

Spiritual appetite can be distressing, but you won't die if you don't satisfy it.

Spiritual hunger is more desperate, but it's better for our practice because it tends to deactivate the discriminating mind. We feel it so intensely that we simply have to eat what's there. Zazen nourishes our hunger by pointing to the "food" of the present moment. Without zazen we don't see that we are continuously being sustained by the changing, interdependent world. Zazen is both means and end. As Dogen says in the *Genjokoan*, "Zazen is enlightenment; enlightenment is zazen." Zazen provides the single-minded focus on what's going on right now: handing five dollars to the homeless man on the beach, helping your child with her homework, answering the phone, hanging a picture on the wall. Zazen allows us to root out the ignorance nourishing our belief that only something out of the ordinary will satisfy our spiritual hunger. It's the same ignorance that sustains the "thirst" of the three poisons of greed, hatred, and ignorance. This thirst and spiritual hunger are partners.

The problem isn't eradicating hunger so much as it is finding nourishment. To be alive is to be hungry. So there are no intellectual solutions to the problem, only existential ones. In other words, we can only feed our spiritual hunger by living, being, doing. Peace of mind is not removed from our world of starvation and homelessness. Nor is it removed from our delight in its beauty and bounty. When we realize the ordinary moment as nourishment, we have truly found our long lost home. Our hunger is appeased and there is peace of mind. It may sound like a contradiction, but there really is peace in the midst of all the motion, change, and tension of our lives. It's best encapsulated by the lovely Buddhist metaphor of the lotus in the midst of fire. Picture that. Opening yourself to the moment is living like the lotus, surrounded everywhere by flames yet indestructible through it all. There is no way of intellectually reconciling the contradictions of purity and filth, knowledge and ignorance, pleasure and pain. This can only come about experientially.

We need spiritual hunger as a steady reminder to practice. This longing for peace of mind directs us to zazen. It reminds us that we have to make an effort to sit, to keep our practice alive, not to prove anything to anyone (not even to ourselves) but to live up to our potential as human beings. Peace of mind is our birthright. Like blades of grass turning toward the sun, we find peace of mind by turning toward the moment, toward life.

TIDES OF THE SPRING SEA,

TIDE AFTER INDOLENT

TIDE

DRIFTING ON AND ON . . .

BUSON

EVERYTHING JUST IS

MAKING THINGS HAPPEN

It's very difficult for us to allow life to go "drifting on and on," to stream along, experiencing ourselves as no different from "tide after indolent tide." We are suspicious of drifters. We are obsessed, in fact, with being actors, makers, bosses. When we call someone a "doer," we're giving that person a compliment. We get very huffy when our exertions come to nothing or when the purpose of our activity turns out completely contrary to what we had in mind.

There's a New Age notion that we can create or "discreate" our own fates, manipulate or control events. It's all mind over matter. Create your own success. Discreate your cancer. Manage your mind into perfect health, wealth, and happiness. And if you fail? Well, then you must not have tried hard enough. Some people mistakenly believe that Zen falls into this category. They come to the practice thinking it will turn their lives around or that they'll develop the power of mind to "make things happen." Why practice Zen if you aren't going to be able to shape your life according to your own ideal situation?

It's hard for people when they first come to Zen to understand that you can sit just to sit—that there's no goal for "bettering" your situation, your life, or yourself. When they ask us why we sit, we tell them that we practice Zen because we're *living* Zen. It's not a metaphor or a symbol or a means toward something other than Zen, nor does it implicitly contain a promise that something good will come to us as a reward. Sitting, as one of our Zen teachers used to say, is "just sitting for its own sake." And living is just living for its own sake. No ornamentation. No visualizing great things. No big bang that will transform you from being short and fat into being tall and thin. When you're sitting and your toes cramp up, you aren't trying to eliminate the painful experience by "breathing it away," or "discreating" it through positive thinking, or "transcending" it. You're just cramping.

Those who remain with us after we've given that explanation go on to ask, "How, then, do we make things happen? How do we get hold of our lives and put them on course?" This is a typical Western misinterpretation of sitting as an action that leads somewhere. It's unthinkable that anyone would indulge in such a boring, painful exercise for hours on end unless there were some spectacular result.

Another typical Western misinterpretation of Zen is that it's a form of Asian fatalism, or that there's some inscrutable motive behind it—maybe discovering supernatural secrets, like learning about past lives or becoming a sage by tapping into the universal "energy flow." Then there are the self-help people who see it as a form of inspirational relaxation. "Oh, I see, you're sitting so you can learn to just stop and smell the roses and not be such a workaholic, right?"

THE ART OF DOING NOTHING

In practicing Zen, we're not making anything happen. We're becoming one with the active, dynamic living event that is this very moment, whether it's roses or cancer or rainfall. We are motion, but not the mover. We're being receptive without being passive. Being open, being one with the moment doesn't allow any space for a passive receiver and an active supplier. There are no two events happening, only one experience, one moment; then another experience appearing as the next moment; and the next, and the next, and the next . . . continuously changing experiences coming and going as moments rise and fall. This movement is beautifully illustrated by the rising and falling of the breath. We don't have to make the breath happen; it happens by itself. In sitting, where we become one with the natural rise and fall of the breath, we are closest to our true nature—the effortlessly flowing stream of life itself. There's no one outside to stop and comment on the stream, to divert it, to fish in it, or to drink it; there's just breathing *as* the stream of life itself.

When you live with this awareness, there's no fretting about making this or that happen or go away. Take, for example, sitting up in bed in the morning, putting on socks, and applying the same awareness to putting on socks as you give to following your breath on your cushion. There's just your arm moving, the feel of the sock pulling up over your foot, the arch of your neck as you bend over. Thinking of nothing at all, putting every bit of yourself into simply pulling on that sock. Suddenly the world opens up. There's an enormous rush of joy for no reason at all. Everything outside you and inside you is swallowed up by that sock going over your toes. It all happens so fast, you can't even say how long the moment lasts. There's not even any sense of you pulling on the sock. It could just as easily be the sock pulling you on. You and your sock and your foot and your elbow and your neck have somehow all vanished into the act itself. It's not that you physically disappear or go into some altered state; it's just that you've dropped into the pure joy of closing the gap between yourself and the moment of pulling on your sock.

Sure, there's an intention: putting on your socks. Going to the drawer, taking out the socks, sitting down on the bed: every one of those gestures is expressing life at that moment, expressing this particular bodymind complex in motion—dressing, walking to and from the bed to the drawer. Millions and millions of little neurological impulses move you along, muscular activity manifesting as thoughts impelling you; nanoseconds of thought after thought go into that procedure.

When we are open, flowing, moving without thinking self-consciously, fully one with the moving moment, there is no dualistic push and pull between the maker and the object yielding to the maker's will. There's no self thinking of itself pulling on a sock. There's simply the moment of "dressing." Isn't it a pity how "making things happen" distracts us? It distracts us from the absolute perfection of the moment, unadorned and radiant just as it is.

DISAPPEAR INTO THE MOMENT

As long as we have the sense of a self that is busily setting about ordering things, we'll be frustrated. It's when we're not on top of things but at one with them, that we awaken to the true nature of the self.

What is the right time to make something happen? What is the wrong time? Who knows? There's only this time, this moment. Settle into this moment of breathing, of putting on socks, of cooking. Of course we will make plans for and have thoughts of the future—it's not as if we cut ourselves off from the planning mind.

It's okay to find yourself thinking about that vacation coming up in two weeks; it's okay to picture yourself setting up the tent in the mountains. It makes you feel good for a moment, but then let those thoughts float through you without latching on to them. Then come back—to putting on this sock, stirring this pot of spaghetti, reading this book. Without having to create or discreate it, let yourself truly disappear into the moment.

STRIVING AND PERSISTING

SELFISH STRIVING

It may appear that our grassroots practice elevates "being" above "doing," but that's not the case. To clarify this, let's take another look at the great Indian epic, the *Bhagavadgita*. The central issue of the story is a decision that must be made by Arjuna, a royal warrior. He is sitting on a hill overlooking the field of battle, contemplating his entry, knowing that if he goes down to fight, he'll have to kill people, some of whom are his royal relatives, members of his own family. A dialogue begins between Arjuna and his charioteer, Krishna, one of the manifestations of the Hindu god Vishnu. The topic is caste duty. As a member of the warrior caste, Arjuna's duty is to fight and kill, no matter how he feels about it.

Orthodox Hindu interpretations of the story claim that through his dialogue with Krishna, Arjuna comes to understand that he has to live up to his caste duty. But Mahatma Gandhi came up with his own radical interpretation of the *Bhagavadgita*. He saw the entire dialogue as a psychological and emotional battle within—an exercise in becoming selfless, giving up desires, no longer striving for greatness, power, or glory, and thereby achieving spiritual liberation.

As a Buddhist practice, Zen is grounded in Indian religious tradition. But what do these religious interpretations of desire, striving, and selflessness have to do with Grassroots Zen? Is it really reasonable for any Western spiritual practice to demand that we give up striving or that we abandon our goals, ideals, and aspirations?

Spiritual striving is like spiritual hunger. We feel that something is missing and are driven to find out what it is. Hoping to ease our minds, we put our "goldfish bowl on the path and run to a fire." We soon learn that our striving takes two forms: one attempts to escape change and has a blind belief in an abiding self. It yearns for eternal youth, recognition, power, glory, money, and fame. This striving is nothing but the attempt to build up a permanent structure of the ego, aggrandizing the self and overshadowing others. As the Buddha pointed out, the very foundation of this kind of striving is ignorance of the true nature of the self as transient, flexible, dynamic, and, most of all, impermanent. This isn't to say that the self is unreal. As we've pointed out a number of times, the self is not illusory but insubstantial, always changing. It's like a cloud moving across the sky, delivering rain or snow, and an occasional tornado, but never abiding. It's always changing color, form, speed, and motion.

Striving based on ignorance of the true transitory nature of the self is the same as attachment. It's the ego's thirst for invulnerability and immortality. In Zen practice as we've come to understand it, this form of striving has to be faced and acknowledged rather than abandoned. We have to keep an eye on it, but that doesn't mean we can get rid of it. It's there, it's part of us, so trying to get rid of it would be like a dog trying to catch its own tail. Keeping an eye on the ego's desire for permanence lets us see how ridiculous and useless it is. Our awareness discloses how selfish striving inevitably brings about the very suffering it's seeking to avoid. The best we can do is acknowledge it, pay attention to our selfish striving in the same way we observe the rising and falling of the breath. Paying attention is itself a way of inviting change. It provides the knowledge that dispels the ignorance fueling the fire of striving. Carrying that attention from our cushions into our everyday lives, we get to know more about the real nature of the self. Gradually, without developing the striving to overcome striving, we transform its pernicious nature.

SELFLESS STRIVING

The second form of striving is related to the bodhisattva ideal of the person who postpones her own liberation in order to help others. This is the kind of selflessness Gandhi was talking about. It involves action, realizing an ideal. Selfless striving requires immersing oneself in the world of the many beings. It's a form of karma yoga, the practice of action. Here the self is lost in the process of becoming one with an action. The difference between this selfless striving and its selfish twin is that it's not engaged in enhancing the permanence of the self. In moving away from that demarcated, individual self and becoming one with others, it erases the borders of dualism and distinction.

Selfless striving is a form of desire best personified by Kannon, the bodhisattva of compassion. Synonymous with empathy and love, compassion grows with listening to the sounds of the world and tuning in to the voices of the many beings. We're not talking about the grand acts of self-sacrifice you read about in heroic epics like the *Bhagavadgita*. Kannon is more ordinary than that. Instead of thunderbolts and swords, she carries tools and utensils—hammers, brooms, buckets, ladles, spinning wheels—that symbolize actions we perform every day. Kannon's tools represent the entire canvas of human existence, which, over time, is filled with the myriad hues, shapes, and forms of selfless striving.

THE ART OF DOING SOMETHING

In real-life situations, it's hard to distinguish between the two forms of striving. We have to be modest in order to honestly observe our own tendencies. Honesty and truthfulness are the tools and utensils of our practice. We especially need them when we're sitting with selfish striving. We may see things about ourselves that we don't want to see, and there's always the temptation to turn away. So we must be vigilant.

It helps to remember that we're searching for the *true* self, not just the self. What exactly is this true self? We don't know, but we still find the word "true" meaningful. It indicates that we have to drop our masks and bear witness to *all* our strivings if we want to transform selfishness into selflessness. Striving for truth is a good way of distinguishing between them. But be forewarned, this is no abstract intellectual exercise. We don't want to drive ourselves crazy labeling every single manifestation of striving. "Oh, was that one 'selfless' or 'selfish?'" Not at all. We're talking about being with the striving as it comes up, and then letting it go. Once we do that, striving will manifest itself as compassion. We can't push it or force it to happen. But if we become one with this very moment, the true self will shine forth on its own. It will appear as the striving to hear the sounds of the world and help the many beings.

PERSISTENCE

Unlike patience, which is the ability to wait, persistence is the ability to go on despite obstacles on the path. It's more in keeping with the "doing" aspect of our practice. Meeting and overcoming challenges requires that we be active and muster the courage to carry on despite boredom, staleness, and all the other problems besetting us from "inside" and "outside." Persistence is the determination to go on sitting when we feel we aren't getting anywhere. We talked about spiritual staleness earlier in the book. This is a slightly different take on the subject.

One day we might find ourselves asking, "Why am I doing this? I've heard it over and over again and it's always the same—the importance of zazen, of being one with the moment, of watching the breath, of letting inside and outside become one. There's nothing new happening. Why should I persist?" When we let this voice take over, we're being led around by circumstances. We're simply reacting to environmental stimuli, seeking fugitive pleasures, making things easy on ourselves. After a couple of months, we grow bored with the pleasures we've exchanged for zazen. Again we feel we're missing something. We feel homesick. No surprise, considering that it was the longing for our true home that brought us to Zen in the first place.

Giving up is not a viable alternative to persistence. Giving up takes precious time away from working on ourselves. We're so fortunate to be able to sit zazen in a safe place, surrounded by dharma friends, and without worrying about starving to death. To be cavalier about it, to waste the window of karmic opportunity would be a shame. Who knows when it will come back again?

Persistence is the virtue of listening to the voice that deters us from practice, of noting where it's coming from, and at the same time, sympathetically but firmly moving it out of the way. Persistence is the courage to acknowledge that there will always be moments when we feel like giving up. Like emotion, slackening is also part of being human. We're not here to punish ourselves. Our practice isn't about developing the monstrous guilt complex that too often masquerades as spirituality. We can accept the fact that it's sometimes hard to cut through the mind's chatter. We never said that returning to the moment would always be easy. Yet persistence makes it possible to acknowledge the present distraction without giving in to it. All we need is three or four minutes of real effort, of following the breath, and that voice begins to fade. As we meet the moment in the rhythm of our breath, we feel a great weight being lifted from our hearts.

EMBRACING OBSTACLES

There's a very loving element to persistence when we embrace our obstacles. We might resist at first. Who wants to shake hands with the enemy? Yet zazen provides a proper framework for doing just that. Persistence offers the knowledge that reluctance isn't our enemy; it's only another condition, a life experience. It's like the self—also a passing condition—very real but passing nonetheless. Persistence allows us to be easy with that passing condition and to dance with our life-moments. Sometimes that dance will exhaust us and sometimes we'll just glide along. The steps and partners, the rhythm and music will always be different, but we'll go right on dancing. Through the dark shadows of boredom and despair, we'll persist in our practice.

OUR BEST SEASON

THE MIND AT EASE

When there's no fixed self carrying around a huge bundle of likes and dislikes, every season is our best season. Still, putting down that bundle, even for a short while, is no simple task. Let's say we like summer and dislike winter. It's hard to imagine ourselves going out in a blizzard and gleefully "bringing inside a lovely bright ball of snow." Yet as the Buddha pointed out, the more summer we want, the more winter we get. We're frustrated because we aren't authoring our life's script. If we had it our way, there'd be no winter, no isolation, no difficulty, no death.

Zazen is our "Hello!" It's our call to "Light the fire!" It enjoins us to truly enjoy life not only while sitting and consciously following the breath, but also while performing our everyday routines in our environment of the moment—regardless of the season. In this state of bare attention, just putting up the storm windows brings us into harmony with winter.

THE ZEN OF GARDENING

Being human, we'll never entirely give up our likes and dislikes. If you love strawberry ice cream, don't think you'll become enlightened if you switch to chocolate because you heard that a great Zen master loves chocolate ice cream. Such misguided thinking has prompted many a Zen enthusiast into all sorts of strange behaviors. As novices, we, too, thought that copying our teachers was part of Zen practice. One of them smoked a lot. We'd given up smoking long before, but we'd sit with him, smoking one cigarette after the next, thinking that smoking had something to do with the fact that he knew all the answers to all 1700 koans in the Rinzai-Zen curriculum. Maybe smoking had a "mystical" component to it. Maybe it was a "special teaching" directed just at me!

In the 1970s and 1980s, many intelligent people went off with teachers who not only smoked and drank excessively but also sexually abused them. Mistaking license for detachment, many seekers actually believed that, as "enlightened beings," their teachers were above and beyond cancer and liver disease, not to mention ethics. Unfortunately, some of them still believe this.

There's a difference between taking license and being in your best season, that is, not being dragged around when things don't go your way. Life provides countless opportunities for developing this kind of detachment. What happens, for example, when you work very hard on a project for a long time and it goes nowhere, or when you do all the right things and everything turns out wrong? Although we don't garden, we have close friends who do. Caring for their vegetables and flowers when they were away disclosed similarities between gardening and responding to such situations. Here are the three most important ones:

1. Setting your will against circumstances is like trying to push a seedling to grow faster, hoping it will produce fruit or vegetables earlier. This is a sure way to stunt its growth.

2. Maintaining vigilance is important, but watch out for over-kill. (A case in point: To protect their plants from aphids, farmers in Central Illinois sent in an army of ladybugs last summer—only to find themselves faced later with an exploding population of ladybugs. As late as November, ladybugs were everywhere: in sofas, pantries, drawers, and beds. We even found some crawling around in our socks!)

3. If you're totally wrapped up in reaping the harvest, you can't lose yourself in the work of the moment.

ON BELIEVING IN MIND

The fourth Chinese Zen ancestor composed a simple but pro-found poem called "*Hsin Hsin Ming*," which means "On Believing in Mind." He wrote, "The more you try to stop motion in order to attain rest, the more your rest becomes rest-lessness." Forgetting, stopping, letting go—all this calls for us to stop trying to author the script of our lives. It's a daunting prospect, particularly for Americans, who've been taught from early childhood that "your life is what you make it." In our society, few people know the importance of getting out of the way and letting creativity take over. We ought to listen more to artists who tell us that it's only when they stop controlling the process of painting or dancing or writing that these come of themselves. It's simply a question of trust, of believing in the true self.

In Zen painting, the artist vanishes and "bamboo paints bamboo." The picture may not always turn out beautifully; it may even end in failure. But for the Zen artist, even failure can become a source of liberation. Koans, too, are an art form. They're meant to be lived, not collected and stuck away in dusty libraries. As we see them, koans are the energy, the very stuff of our daily experience. They reflect our joys and sorrows, our play and our work. We're constantly grappling with life koans: losing ourselves in daily life activities and situations as, more and more, we come to believe in the true self.

Like life, koans are often paradoxical. For example, how do we go about "losing" the self to find the true self? Do we have to erase all thoughts and feelings? How do we shut out the noise of life? Wrestling with these questions intellectually quickly gets us nowhere. We simply have to sit with them until we *become* them. The answers are everywhere, beckoning to us in the air we breathe and in the sound of the repairman's hammer next door. There is no rarefied other place where we'll find that true self, only the one right here, manifesting in that clacking hammer.

Believing in the true self means experiencing the self as the universe of sound, air, and breath. We constantly move between interdependence and distinction, juggling our selfish and selfless strivings with every breath we take. To plug into the process, catch your response to the image of a genocidal dictator as it flashes across the TV screen. How can this man call himself a human being? What gives him the right to condemn thousands of people to death? Then recognize how you're doing exactly that. Perched on your lofty throne of self-right-eousness, you're condemning that man to death. As soon as you see this, there's no longer a gap between you and the man you're despising. You're both capable of the same hatred. This is not to say that you're embracing his cause, or that you don't want to see him brought to justice. Abandoning moral respon-sibility isn't the way to interdependence. But neither is setting yourself apart from others—no matter how abhorrent they may be. Living interdependence doesn't mean becoming a marshmallow and never taking a position. But there's no set of rules or regulations on this one. No daily list of merits and demerits to check off. There's only the practice of carrying your awareness into action.

PRACTICING WITH THE WORLD OF THE TEN THOUSAND THINGS

The world of the ten thousand things is breathing along with us as we sit on our cushions. It doesn't stop because we've stopped. It's just that we slow down our hyperactive minds in response to that world and recognize ourselves as part of it all—from the tiniest insect chirping in the garden to the full moon shining in the night sky. In zazen, we make time and space for stopping to acknowledge what's going on all the time: life. And since life starts with the breath, we begin by focusing on our breath.

Instead of using the intellect to analyze ways in which we can experience interdependence, we allow ourselves to sink into the experience of the moment without thinking about it. For example, if we allow ourselves to simply see the image without commenting, watching that dictator on TV can itself become an occasion for experiencing interdependence. It's like experiencing the moment of the repairman's clacking hammer next door when you're sitting zazen; you're hearing the sound but not following a train of thoughts about it.

Living interdependence means seeing people where they are, not where we'd like them to be. A good example of this is the Dalai Lama's relationship to the Chinese who are responsible for mass killings in Tibet. He's deeply pained by their actions, yet he doesn't hate them. Coming from the experience of interdependence, he sees them as no different from himself, yet he knows that they're not yet ready to acknowledge this from their end. He knows that you can only take people so far, that you can't push them to do the right thing when the time isn't right. Still that doesn't keep him from trying, from spreading his message of peaceful coexistence.

The next time you see that dictator on TV, give him your full attention. If you can find the whole world reflected in his eyes, you'll know what interdependence is. From that space, you can move on to action: demonstrate, hold up a sign, endorse a nonviolent way to force the dictator to step down. Experiencing interdependence doesn't mean the end of political vigilance; it is, instead, the beginning of social responsibility.

FORBEARANCE

FATALISM

All religious traditions have ways of dealing with adversity. Each provides its own "small island" for those who are "lost at sea." In the West, some call this island "forbearance." We have been raised to see the awful, difficult, or unpleasant events in our lives as tests: tests of our goodness, of our ability to bow in the face of God's will. The greater our forbearance, the greater our capacity for spiritual understanding. But ours is an active forbearance; there is always the gritting of teeth and bucking up against it. There's a bit of aggression in that, and it often comes out in the form of intolerance. For centuries, we've waged wars to get others to forbear under the yoke of our particular version of God. The East, too, has seen its share of religious warfare. But people there are generally raised to be more passive in the face of personal adversity.

Traveling to countries like India, the home of the Buddha, is an opportunity for understanding the conflicted feelings of many Western Buddhists. Seeing people sitting at the banks of the Ganges, sick and starving, is a shock to those of us who've been raised to "get going when the going gets tough." There's something terrible about this kind of giving in. Why aren't these people doing something, why are they knuckling under to circumstances with such smiling acceptance? Why do they justify their inaction by saying, "Once this particular karma has run its course, I will do better in another incarnation"? That's fatalism.

There's much fatalism in popular Buddhism, for example, in the salvation sects of the Pure Land, where the alleviation of suffering is placed in the hands of Amidha Buddha, a Christ-like figure of redemption. Pure Land Buddhists pray to this Buddha to bring them to the "Western paradise" after they die. In the past, several Japanese Zen masters spoke out against this popular movement, chastising its priests for promoting fatalism. With its emphasis on individual experience and avoidance of intermediaries, Zen appears to be very similar to our own individualistic approach to spirituality. But that's only at first glance.

The form of Japanese Zen that came to the West emphasized unquestioning obedience on the part of the student. Although it discouraged dependence on the Buddha, it nonetheless imposed its strict Confucian cultural norms on an extremely individualistic population of spiritual seekers. Ironically, by submitting to their Zen masters' beatings, humiliations, and autocratic pronouncements in the name of "real Zen training," Western Zen practitioners turned forbearance into fatalism.

HONING AWARENESS

You don't have to be from the East or the West to skirt the confrontation with suffering; you simply have to be human.

There are innumerable ways of avoiding the "great matter" of life and death, spirituality being one of the best. We use it to become slaves to form, to religious ritual, to obedience or rebellion. We talk about practice more than we actually do it. Skirting the real issue, we escape from reality into fantasy. It doesn't matter whether we push up against life's challenges with forbearance or fatalistically await redemption. In either case, we're avoiding that unadorned confrontation with suffering.

We consider our meeting with ts'ao-pen ch'an to be very fortuitous. The old Chinese grassroots practitioners were earthy and practical. Not being particularly religious, they took all the metaphysical references out of Buddhism and replaced them with images from daily life. It's not that they suffered less, but they honed their awareness of suffering on the whetstone of activity. They were radical in their refusal to see adversity as anything other than the Buddha. Their nondualistic vision of life probably came from Chinese Taoism, with its emphasis on nature. This combination of Buddhism and Taoism resulted in their understanding of Zen as a dynamic activity that was no different from the cycles of life.

This kind of grassroots awareness reveals that there is no solid adversity to buck up against. There is no supreme being up there handing out good and bad karma. This is it. Right here, the Tao is manifesting itself—as suffering, as laughing, as breathing, as walking. Note that these are all i-n-g words; they are gerunds, words of action, events taking place now, in the present moment, not in the past and not in the future. There is nothing but flowing motion. When adversity appears, Buddha appears. And that's all there is. The gap between you and adversity is closed. Nothing remains but the dynamic energy of the event. Soon the event itself disappears, giving way to a new manifestation of energy in motion. This is not escaping into paradise. Paradise is right here, manifesting as suffering.

Life gives us no end of opportunities for honing awareness. Adversities, too, are occasions for deepening insight, but not by forbearing against them. If we do that, we're resisting, splitting off from them. That's when it appears that there's somebody up there throwing down one test after another at us. What can we do but placate this powerful force or knuckle under and show it how good we are? Or maybe we have no part in the process and it's just karma.

There is a famous koan about a monk who was turned into a fox for teaching that enlightened people evaded the law of cause and effect. Clearly, that's a very one-sided view of enlightenment. But in a way, the enlightened person is different from others because instead of forbearing against her karma, she leaps right into it. She is it. In leaping in and becoming one with it, she neutralizes it—the adversity as well as the pleasure flowing along as cause and effect. There is joy in this great leap. It's the joy of recognizing that adversity is coming and going as the transient bodymind we call the self.

Grassroots Zen is about practicing in every condition and in all situations. There is neither forbearance nor fatalism in this kind of practice. We do it by breathing, feeling, thinking, loving, living, and transforming. These activities comprise the field of our practice. The more rooted in this awareness, the more flexible and accepting we become. No rigid submission to fate, this free-flowing acceptance is indistinguishable from the law of cause and effect.

THE MAGIC OF THE MUNDANE

Zen teacher Thich Nhat Hanh says that you can't meditate on a cushion if you can't meditate while doing the dishes. He's repeating what old master Chao-Chou said when a novice came and asked if he could study with him. "Have you eaten your rice yet?" Chao-Chou asked. "Yes," answered the monk. "Then go wash your bowl," said Chao-Chou. Interview over. If you can find "holiness" in the most mundane activity, you're practicing Zen. From there, it's only a small step to finding it in adversity. Let's go back to the Dalai Lama's situation. A reporter once asked him, "How do you feel about Mao Tse-tung?" The answer came quickly: "Mao Tse-tung is also the Buddha." It would be easy to interpret that as the saintly ability to forgive your enemy. But it isn't. The Dalai Lama's experience of Mao Tse-tung as the Buddha gave the Tibetan leader the opportunity to become one with his tragic karma. It didn't come from communing with angels or the dead spirits of great masters or reincarnations of future Dalai Lamas. It was a matter-of-fact statement of his experience of interdependence.

DETACHMENT AND IMMERSION

It was neither forbearance nor detachment that made Kannon a bodhisattva, but total immersion in the cries of the world. We must do likewise. This is not to say that we become totally mired in the misery around us. Sitting keeps us sane. At the same time, lest we forget, life is always going to tweak our noses. We're always going to find ourselves swinging back and forth between dualism and oneness. It's a tightrope we're constantly walking. To think of ourselves as detached from it all is to negate true Zen experience. That's why the old teachers were so harsh when students came to them boasting of their detachment. Master Lin-chi, for example, was always giving someone a slap to remind him that he wasn't some kind of spirit floating above his body. He was especially harsh with those who considered themselves too holy for this world.

There's social involvement in every Zen story, indicating that we can't even be detached from, for example, the death of a cat. Master Nan-ch'uan, Chao-Chou's teacher, tries to stop a fight over a cat among several monks in his monastery. "If any of you can give me a turning word, I won't cut this cat in half," he shouts. Possibly because the monks aren't too strong in their practice, none comes forth and the cat is cut in two. Later, when Chao-Chou returns to the monastery, Nan-ch'uan tells him what happened. Chao-Chou puts his sandal on his head and walks out the door. Nan-chuan calls after him, "If you were there, the cat would have been spared." What is this but Chao-Chou engaging in the pain of being cut in two?

In the paradoxical way of our practice, we cannot hope to be free of dualism without immersing ourselves fully in the sounds, sights, tastes, pains, and struggles of this world. Although there is no permanent self to experience these, at the same time, real tears are shed and real blood flows. There is no detaching from this fact of life. There is no forbearing against it. There is only this.

SELF-IMPROVEMENT VS. SELF-REALIZATION

UNEARTHING THE ROOT OF SUFFERING

The Buddha likens the true spiritual seeker to someone hit by an arrow. Such a person doesn't stop to ask who made the arrow or who sent it flying or whether it's tipped with poison; all he or she wants is to get it out—now! Most people who come to see what Zen practice is like aren't that desperate. They come because of the nagging feeling that something is missing from their lives, or because they're hurting, or because they want to become better people. Since Grassroots Zen is a worldly practice for ordinary people and not for monks, it doesn't distinguish too much between the two types of seekers. Whatever their reasons for coming, sincere practitioners aren't looking for short-term fixes.

Meditation has become a popular form of alternative medical treatment. We read in today's paper, for example, that one of the biggest health insurers in Illinois is now offering coverage to patients who use meditation for a variety of physical and mental conditions. We have nothing against these practical goals. Charitable goals are fine too. Meditation is being used in prisons and in peace and reconciliation groups to help people become less violent, more loving, more tolerant. But this isn't what we offer. Zazen is our grassroots way. Instead of using it to deal with problems, we cultivate the "voiceless flower" that "speaks to the obedient in-listening ear." This is another way of saying we're directing our efforts to self-realization rather than to self-improvement.

There's a difference between meditating to achieve an immediate goal, like becoming a healthier or a better person, and committing yourself to a lifetime of zazen practice with no tangible goal at all. Yasutani Hakuun Roshi once described the two kinds of people who come to Zen as those seeking a temporary cure for suffering and those seeking to unearth the root of suffering altogether. Although he didn't brush aside the former, he pointed out that this instrumental attitude wasn't enough to sustain a long-term relationship with Zen, one that goes beyond simply adding another "technique" to our first-aid kit.

Looking to Zen for self-improvement isn't an American invention. It has a long tradition in Japan that goes back to its ancient warrior society. Most samurai used Zen, in fact, to become more skilled at making war and dying. They practiced zazen in order to develop better concentration so they would be better swordsmen and less fearful in facing an enemy. Today Japanese businesspeople use it to become more concentrated competitors. The impulse of the businesspeople does not differ much from that of the samurai. The motivation for self-improvement takes many forms.

The second group of people who come to Zen—those who Yasutani Hakuun Roshi described as seeking to unearth the root of suffering altogether—aren't any less troubled or pained than the first. Often, in the course of training, those

seeking self-improvement develop into committed Zen practitioners while the so-called "spiritual" seekers disappear. The
issue is not so much the reasons for coming as what happens
once you actually sit down and start to meditate. You might
come wanting to improve yourself and leave after six sessions
because you feel you aren't getting anywhere. Likewise, you
can be driven by a profound, lifelong existential question, and
also leave after those same six sessions for the same reason. The
important thing is to stick to the practice no matter what.
You've got to develop the love of sitting for its own sake—and
an appreciation for paradox, because the point of Zen is seeing
that there isn't any static self to improve or realize!

MISTAKEN NOTIONS

Everyone comes to practice with mistaken notions. Ours centered on the idea of enlightenment. It took a long time to wear
down this obstacle and to see that enlightenment can be just
another way of glorifying the self. Even thinking about this self
that wants to be enlightened is being dragged around by it.
There's no end to its neediness. Spiritual or physical, it doesn't
make any difference. No matter how good or worthy the cause,
it's still a diversion from the moment, from the immediate
experience of what's going on right now.

We are overtaken by the need to acquire something we
think we don't have yet.

This attitude is deeply engrained in the American consciousness. Take Benjamin Franklin's *Autobiography*, that staple of
high school reading. Franklin is the model for all would-be
"self-made" men and women. He leaves home to acquire a better life for himself: an education, a profession that will bring
him more money, respect and admiration from the community
as well as knowledge of nature, of science, of people. So he

makes a self-improvement chart listing the traits he wants to develop—charity, temperance, humility, modesty, and so on—and he checks off his progress every day.

An interesting contrast in attitudes is the autobiography of Franklin's Japanese contemporary, the Zen poet Bashō, who lists everything he wants to get rid of as he leaves home on his journey of self-discovery. There aren't any stated goals in Basho's book, only a simple account of the experience of living. He is completed not by the acquisition of virtue but by feeling the rain on his face during a spring shower.

The moment of self-improvement is a self-conscious moment. There's no room for experience because the self is taking up every inch of space. For example, in musing about modesty, Ben Franklin loses the possibility for being modest under a heap of notions about modesty. He distances himself from it by thinking about it; whereas Bashō embodies it in his experience of the spring rain. There's no end to self-improvement because there's no end to analyzing all our faults and good points, to weighing and measuring them in our search for that perfect balance.

For lack of a better word, the "goal" of Zen has less to do with acquiring even good qualities than with sitting itself. There may be positive by-products of the practice that improve our life situations, but there may not, or they may not be as quickly apparent as we'd like. But we shouldn't forget that these are only by-products. We know people who've been practicing for over fifty years, and they don't strike us as being very "self-improved" as a result. Very few of them, in fact, would win a popularity contest. But Zen isn't about winning popularity contests or becoming a saint. You don't go into it with a checklist. Sure, there's the underlying goal of awakening to something you don't see right now, something you sense will alleviate that undercurrent of discontent. But you don't want to get caught by the mistaken notion that you're sitting in order to become enlightened, because that's only a subtler and more obstructive longing for self-improvement.

UNBURDENING

Zen master Dogen criticized the game of one-upmanship that koan practice had become in the Japanese monasteries of his time. He publicly lambasted ambitious monks for using it to aggrandize themselves. Some were even going so far as to "buy" official sanction to teach from their Zen masters. It's still done today:"How many koans did you pass?""I did fifty.""Oh yeah, I only got through twenty." It's a lot like being at the gym and hearing,"I did fifty bench presses yesterday. How many can you do?" Like everything else that pumps up the self, koans, too, can become part of the game. Instead of unburdening ourselves, we keep acquiring, until finally, we've smothered the possibility for seeing the true nature of the naked, unobstructed self.

Nothing makes Zen practice more painful than wanting. But long years of sitting really do become precious in and of themselves, and the wanting fades. Ultimately, we sit just to sit. For example, we no longer come to sesshin hoping to find something we've been missing; we just come to sesshin. For some strange reason, it's all we need. Early in our practice, we anticipate the prospect of something "big" happening during sesshin. A little later on, all we anticipate is pain, boredom, and the cynical certainty that "nothing" will happen. After years, we no longer anticipate anything. As one of our Japanese Zen teachers used to tell reluctant participants who bombarded him with questions about what it would be like, "Sesshin is sesshin. You come, you find out."

Zazen is a wonderful opportunity for unburdening ourselves of the desire for self-improvement. Just feeling the rain on your face as you walk out the zendo door is enough.

PASSION IN COMPASSION

BODHISATTVA ACTIVITY

Many people think of compassion as a kind of band-aid to plaster over meanness. But we see compassion as wisdom, the opposite of ignorance. In Buddhism, compassion is the very nature of bodhisattva activity. It's not a question of cultivating compassion in response, or as a palliative to the evil actions borne of greed, hatred, and ignorance. Patching up lapses in wisdom aren't what we're talking about here. Compassion can't be imposed or self-consciously performed from the outside. It's an organic development, the natural growth of wisdom that comes with practicing zazen.

We've alluded to the prevailing misconception of Zen as a passionless way of relating to life, a detachment that borders on fatalism. It's a preconception we have about what it is to be "a beggar naked except for his robes of heaven and earth!" We literally think we have to be nondescript "beggars," that by erasing every bit of individuality, we'll achieve some colorless ideal of "no self." Grassroots practitioners also fall into this trap. As soon as we start sitting, we think we'll get rid of our obtrusive personalities. Many Western Zen groups have open meetings, consciousness-raising sessions where people wrestle with such problems. Anger is an especially hot topic at the Zen centers we've been to. We encourage open discussions related to practice in our zendo, but we steer away from group therapy.

There's a tendency in psychologically-oriented Zen students to want to remove any vestige of "juiciness" or eccentricity from their practice. They often justify this tendency by citing a famous line from a koan by Zen Master Chao-Chou: "The enlightened mind avoids picking and choosing." Like so many koans, however, this one is not to be taken as a religious axiom or a commandment—"Thou shalt not pick and choose"—but as a living expression of bodhisattva activity. The mind that stops picking and choosing is dead, incapable of activity of any kind. As long as the mind is alive, it's going to keep picking and choosing. Every breath, every thought is a moment of energy and passion in motion. There's no neutral steady-state on any level of human functioning.

REAL-LIFE ZEN

What about those wonderful moments on the cushion that don't seem available at those times in our lives when it's impossible to feel or act like a bodhisattva because we're so filled with rage or hurt or pain? Forgetting that this very body is the Buddha and that this ordinary mind is the Tao, we split off "practice" from "real life."

Real-life Zen practice isn't a sterile void; it's filled with passion for living. This is graphically depicted by the pot-bellied, laughing Hotei, the bodhisattva of the marketplace, who wanders about distributing gifts from his big sack. That's the passionate engagement of the Grassroots Zen practitioner. It's not a license to commit mayhem or let the self run wild, but there is an element of intense feeling that rises naturally when we are totally in sync with the experience of the moment. We mustn't mistakenly toss out this passion that unites us with life, messy and sprawling as it is.

In this sense, passion is the same as selflessness. It comes with the kind of love that attaches us to the earth, to life, to people, stones, weeds, animals, and trees. It makes us *feel*. For the sheer joy of it, like the wise Zen clown Pu-Hua, we want to turn cartwheels in the street.

Real-life Zen practice is the opposite of asceticism. We don't sit to rid ourselves of "earthiness" and "impurity" but, like master Yun-men, to find Buddha in a "shit-stick." We cultivate the passion that goes into caring for something, whether it be a poem, a soufflé, or a street kitten. Every time we refuse to run from the moment—regardless of what it brings—we're engaging compassionately with life. There's nothing bloodless or ascetic about this kind of compassion, but this doesn't mean there won't be times when we feel we're not up to the task. Our jobs may be draining us, we may not be feeling well, those we love may be irritating us, we may suddenly discover we have nothing in common with the people we considered our dearest friends. Any one of these real-life situations has a way of taking the passion out of us. So, what do we do? We plunge into the experience of our situation, become one with it. This in itself is an act of compassion. It's borne of the meditative intensity generated by the regular practice of "letting go."

CRUISING ALONG

Let's say we're cruising along. We're really one with the breath, alert, everything is just fine. Suddenly—BAM!—something happens and we're catapulted out of bliss into misery. Here's the perfect opportunity for recognizing the "interruption" as just another manifestation of "cruising along." Just because it doesn't feel the same doesn't mean that it's come from "out there" to interfere with our practice. Indeed, it's the very vehicle of our practice.

We always laugh at ourselves when we look at pictures taken when we were new to Zen practice. Dressed in black, we were obviously working so hard to look like serious students that we never cracked a smile. That kind of demeanor is what gives Zen a reputation for being "grim." Recently, when a friend from Australia visited with us and we went out together for a beer and a game of billiards, he got all flustered. "I've never been invited out like this with a Zen teacher before," he said. We reminded him of the "Crazy Cloud" Zen masters we'd written about—Lin-chi, Ikkyu, Bankei, and others—whose teaching more often took place in the streets and fields and taverns than in the zendo.

Many of today's grassroots practitioners are still clinging to a monastic inheritance that glorifies the dispassionate attitude of the warrior whose entire life is a preparation for instant death. This may be an appropriate attitude for a warrior, but our grassy field of practice isn't a battlefield. We cultivate life, not death. Our field sits on the interface between them. The melancholy, sweet sadness of our transience must be lived as completely and intensely as the warrior lives his. Yet, unlike the warrior who detaches himself from transience, we must dive right into it.

THE FLOATING WORLD

It isn't "ignorance" when you're fully immersed in the moment-to-moment activities of your life. It's being awake—to the hurt as much as to the joy. Our experience of this "floating world," as the Japanese Buddhists call it, is brief. It's sad. There are no great Zen teachers who haven't commented on this human sadness at passing, because they all felt it themselves. Bankei, for example, was inconsolable at his beloved mother's death. His throat cut during a robbery, the great master Yen-t'ou's dying scream could be heard miles away. In our own time, despite amazing advances in human longevity, technology has only served to emphasize the brevity of life. We see this at the university, where life and human interactions are becoming increasingly "virtual."

We often wonder what people mean when they say, "Get a life!" We have a life, we don't have to get it. There's no need to surf the Web for one. It's right here on our plate. Are we going to just sit and stare at it or count up the calories before daring to eat it? Or do we toss it into the garbage pail, hoping that we'll get something better? It's better to toss out our *ideas* about life and start living it instead. We have to stop psychologizing every little motive and gesture if we want to recapture its spontaneity and passion. After all, do we have a choice?

A friend asked us once why it seemed that the most deeply enlightened Zen teachers often appeared to be cold, somehow "above life." We said that they probably only *appeared* to be untouched. Instead of crying with someone, such a person will exude compassion rather than empathy, and compassion is harder to recognize than the usual kind of commiseration we're accustomed to. It's hard to understand that a Zen teacher isn't holding herself aloof or making a therapeutic effort at avoiding "transference," so we misinterpret stillness as a sign of "coldness." It's better not to worry about other people's degree of enlightenment. It's more important to attend to our own awareness of the moment, of being fully one with pressing the elevator button and saying "Good morning" to our neighbor, of drying the dishes, of pedaling the bike through traffic to work. Nobody lives in perfect awareness all the time; not even the Buddha himself did. But who cares, really? As the Chinese Zen poet Yung-chia put it, "What profit is there in counting your neighbor's treasures?" Without holding ourselves above the fray, it's better to engage in the moment. Such intimacy with the moment eliminates the distinction between the giver and the taker. Just hold that elevator door open, and you're on your way to saving the many beings.

We don't know why the compassion flows or where it's coming from. We simply feel it flowing, taking us in the direction of conserving life, of healing, of stretching out a hand to someone else on the path, a perfect stranger bearing our own face.

ABOUT THE AUTHORS

Manfred B. Steger received his doctorate in political science from Rutgers University. In 1991, together with his wife, Perle Besserman, he founded the Princeton Area Zen Group, where the two are co-teachers. Before coming to Princeton, Steger was a visiting Zen teacher in Hawai'i, Australia, and Europe. In addition to lecturing on Buddhism in the University of Hawai'i system in Honolulu and publishing several articles on lay Zen practice in English and German, he and Perle Besserman coauthored *Crazy Clouds: Zen Radicals, Rebels, and Reformers* (Shambhala, 1991). An associate professor of political science at Illinois State University, Steger is particularly interested in the connection between spirituality and social ethics. His most recent book, on Mahatma Gandhi, is titled *Gandhi's Dilemma: Nonviolent Principles and Nationalist Power* (St. Martin's Press, 2000).

Perle Besserman holds a doctorate in comparative literature from Columbia University and teaches in the English department at Illinois State University. Author of numerous books on spiritual subjects, she has become increasingly interested in women's spirituality and leads various workshops and meditation retreats that seek to incorporate women's wisdom into Zen practice. Her most recent books are *Owning It: Zen and the Art of Facing Life* (Kodansha, 1997), *Teachings of the Jewish Mystics* (Shambhala, 1998), and *The Shambhala Guide to Kabbalah and Jewish Mysticism* (Shambhala, 1998).

The authors' books have been translated into German, Czech, Portuguese, Spanish, Japanese, Italian, Dutch, and Hebrew.